Praise For Magic Words and Language Patterns

At last! Magic Words takes on the subject of hypnotic language with a refreshing ease of use that makes this book stand out for its simplicity. Not only does it present the language plainly, Karen teaches you how to work without scripts, spontaneously and effortlessly in hypnosis and in your life."
~Michael Watson, International NLP and Hypnosis Trainer, award-winning development of "Generative Hypnosis" and Past President of the Hypnosis Education Association

"Get ready to weave a beautiful tapestry of powerful ideas and make all the difference in the world. Karen Hand-Harper's fine book is the magic thread that makes it happen. *Magic Words* is a must read for anyone who wants to really motivate themselves or others."
~Shelley Stockwell-Nicholas, PhD
President of the International Hypnosis Federation

"This book is a must read for anyone who wants to learn how to make the best use of hypnosis and hypnotic techniques. Any serious hypnotist or therapist MUST read this book if they want to expand their influence and help more people. The only problem I have with this book is that I wish I would have written it! By the way, don't just buy this book, utilize every aspect of it!"
~William Horton, Psy.D. MCAP author of *Mind Control, Secret Mind Control*, and *The Secret Psychology of Persuasion*

"Karen offers a dictionary of powerful words and language patterns in an easy to digest method and style. The reader will learn skills that few if any have put into print quite as Karen has. It is easy, informative and Karen anchors skills as she teaches these concepts. I know without a doubt she will receive great praise for a project that has been needed for a long time. I have not read anything as powerful and basic of word skills in hypnosis or, as she enforces, with any and all communication. A great aspect of this book is it will benefit all readers even without

D1591198

hypnosis skills. Karen's book will be a wonderful manual for all CIs to offer their students."
~Larry Garrett, BCH, OB, Owner Garrett Hypnosis and Wellness Center, Chicago

"I love this book. It's captivating, I'm getting so much out of it, and it's so easy to read."
~Erika Flint, BCH, A+Cphi, CEO Cascade Hypnosis Center

"This wonderfully written book has made me aware of just how easily and naturally these "magic words" and language patterns can augment our communication - whether being used in our hypnosis suggestions or in our general everyday lives. Karen has presented the words and patterns in an organized format riddled with examples throughout. Her great sense of humor is reflected on the pages and in her brief stories.
The dependence on scripts takes focus away from clients and the suggestions appropriate to them. Over my years of teaching, I have met many hypnotists and students who were afraid to do 'Scriptless Hypnosis'. Karen's approach stands to be confidence-boosting to the practitioner, by building a simple framework of words and patterns which are simple to follow.

Whether you are new to hypnosis or NLP, or have been using it for years, there are many nuggets to be gained by reading this book. This is an excellent and easy reference which I intend to keep handy in my office and classroom.

Not a hypnotist? No problem. Whether a hypnotist or not, as you absorb the words and patterns Karen Hand-Harper has presented, you will notice an interesting change in your effectiveness of communicating with colleagues, family members, clients and friends.
This book can increase your effectiveness in communicating in every walk of your life and is a must-have for any library."
~Cheryl Elman, CH, CMT, International Hypnosis Trainer

Magic Words
and
Language Patterns

The Hypnotist's Essential Guide to Crafting Irresistible
Suggestions

By

Karen Hand

ReMind Publishing
Chicago, Illinois

Dedication

To Gertrude and Victor Hand for a great start in life;
my husband, Mark A. Harper, for holding on,
encouraging and helping me on our wild and often erratic ride;
and my daughter, Jessica Graham for keeping me inspired to
succeed.

CONTENTS

Foreword

Over my 15 years studying hypnosis, time and again I come across three common trends particularly among new hypnotists: concern over giving the "right" suggestion, belief that the magic is in the words alone, and an obsession with Milton Model language. Each of these trends is detrimental to the hypnotist's skills development. For example, if we look at the idea of the "right" suggestion, often new hypnotists believe that if their suggestions aren't perfectly worded and flow like a hypnotist with years of experience then hypnosis will not work. The hypnotists who fall into this category are those who after an initial consultation scour the internet looking for the perfect script for the client. The unspoken fear is that the hypnotist won't know what to say when the client comes for her or his session.

The second trend is closely related to the first. This is the belief that the client's change is completely reliant on the words the hypnotist uses. For these hypnotists the words and the client's "non-resistance" are the only elements responsible for the change. We know through countless studies that words in reality only make up a tiny part of communication. While they are useful, there are other far more powerful aspects of hypnotherapy, particularly deep rapport and the Placebo Effect.

The final trend is the one I would have been most tempted to fall into in my early days, the obsession with Ericksonian language. Many people who are interested in Milton Erickson's work never move beyond the language patterns that Bandler and Grinder modeled from him. They become so consciously enthralled with the correct pattern names and structures that they treat the Milton Model as being something that is done to a client like a technique instead of seeing the bigger picture that we use this language throughout most of our daily communication. In fact, I've used many of the patterns unconsciously while writing this!

These trends are something that my colleagues and I frequently address when planning our hypnosis trainings, so when I was asked to write the foreword for *Magic Words* I was intrigued with how Karen Hand would present hypnotic language in a way that moved beyond how hypnotic language is typically addressed. Little did I know I was about to read a hypnotic gem. From the first page *Magic Words* is a delightful journey in which the reader is engaged consciously and unconsciously.

From the outset the reader understands that there are no right or wrong words. Instead this book offers the hypnotist a way of understanding language that creates more flexibility and fluidity. The magic of the language presented is not in that it creates the "right" suggestions but that it expands the hypnotist's comfort in working without a script.

Milton Erickson described the root of all problems a client could possibly have is a loss of rapport between the conscious and unconscious mind. Another way of describing this is an incongruence between the conscious and unconscious. One of the key elements to creating an effective session is to model to the client's unconscious mind the desired outcome including states and behaviors throughout the session. For example, when doing an induction, it is the hypnotist's job to model trance for the client. When helping a client to create congruence or rapport between the conscious and the unconscious it is the hypnotist who must model it first. *Magic Words* frees up your conscious mind from needing to read or track suggestions. Instead by being in the right state yourself you can allow these words to connect ideas naturally. The true magic in the language presented in this book is that your sessions become a conversation between two unconscious minds in the most wonderful way.

Magic Words sets itself apart from many other books on hypnotic language because it keeps it simple and applicable immediately. You don't need to be a linguist or have a background in the Milton Model in order to use this book. This is written with ease of use in mind. If you are looking to move beyond scripts, are new to hypnosis, or want to expand your hypnotic language then you will enjoy *Magic Words*. Karen Hand magically weaves language throughout this book so that there are examples for your conscious mind and your unconscious mind. This makes integrating these patterns into your work easy and fun. Karen is a gifted and dynamic hypnotist who brings a charisma that makes these language patterns come to life.

When you are ready to weave magic for your clients while freeing your conscious mind to deeply enjoy the process of helping clients change, move to the next chapter. As you move through these pages, if you should find your relationship with your unconscious mind deepening in ways that allow you to comfortably and naturally speak hypnotically then I certainly couldn't stop you.

Jess Marion
(H)NLP and Hypnosis Trainer
Co-Founder of Theintelligenthypnotist.com

PREFACE

Well, pull up a chair and stick around because this book has a lot more to offer than just words. It has magic and patterns and techniques (Oh my!).

Realize the words and language patterns you are about to discover will have clients (or patients, children, parents, bosses, co-workers, the snooty waiter, etc.) agreeing with your ideas and incorporating them. Your words will resonate and have power. You will be tapping into a deep level of rapport with your listener and receive a new level of success.

You will be able to use these words and patterns while speaking, writing, or posting on social media. And you can effortlessly practice the language strategies in your daily conversations while you watch the difference a turn of words can make to the outcome.

These magic words and language patterns are additional tools for you to add to your tool chest. Before you begin, realize that this book is not designed to teach you how to hypnotize a person. You probably already know how to do that from your certification training. This material is based on Advanced Hypnosis and NLP studies and enough neuroscience to understand how thinking is processed in the brain. And there's a sprinkling of voice and body language insight thrown in for good measure.

You already have everything you need to understand magic words and language patterns. And you will easily incorporate this new information into any technique or pattern or intervention that you already use.

This is not proprietary information for hypnotists alone. Hypnotic language is easily available and useful to doctors, nurses, teachers, caregivers, parents, coaches, chiropractors, acupuncturists, massage therapists, first responders and many others. Once you discover the effectiveness of the patterns, you can imagine the many uses with clients and in your own life.

After getting my college degree in Education and Communications, I spent over 30 years as a radio personality where I had only words as my communication medium. At the same time, I taught radio news writing at Columbia College in Chicago where I helped budding new broadcasters get the most bang out of their buck with the spoken word. For me, words have been the centerpiece for creating a visual image, eliciting a visceral response, and inciting action. Radio personalities are not BROADcasting; they speak one-on-one with the listener. Radio is actually a very individual experience. So, when I became a professional Hypnotist as my second career, it was very natural to use words to motivate individual clients or groups. And once I discovered the magic in certain words and the language patterns that enhance success, I found the word-play thrilling.

It wasn't until after I left radio that I was introduced to Neuro-Linguistic Programming (NLP) and discovered that there is an actual science behind the words and the language patterns that create success. That is what I'm sharing with you here, the science and the magic in the words used for successful communication.

The best part is, you already know the words. So this study becomes a game of using what you already know to increase your success, and not just in client sessions. You will increase success at sales, communication, education, and conversation.

Use these words and patterns to not only effect change in a client, but in all you do; you will have more of an impact in every conversation and situation. That is indeed so much more than "just words!" Let the games begin!

Section 1

HANDBOOK FOR
SCRIPTLESS HYPNOSIS

Chapter 1: Introduction

Have you ever spent valuable time researching and crafting a special script for a client, only to discover during their appointment that there's a bigger issue or a different aspect that has to be addressed first before that script will be useful? Have you found yourself in a panic sending out script requests on social media? Have you combed through the "Big Red Book" of Hypnotic Suggestions and Metaphors by D. Corydon Hammond and still haven't been able to find just the right words that will help your client? Have you wondered if you will ever be experienced enough to help someone change any time/any place without needing a script? First of all, know that you are not alone, and more importantly, imagine how good you will feel when you know just the right words at just the right time!

You are probably already aware that the most respected hypnotists are the ones who can work with anyone and any issue right here and right now. After all, that is what the public expects from a hypnotist. It looks like magical power!

In my first year of practicing hypnosis, I was at a family gathering where friends and relatives were teasingly questioning my sanity about becoming a "witch doctor," the term they thought was so funny. A friend who was about to move to Minnesota shared that he had a fear of driving over bridges. In Chicago, Joe had cleverly mapped routes to avoid all bridges, but that wasn't going to be possible in the Minneapolis/St. Paul area. Joe wondered if I could hypnotize him to get over that fear.

I'd never had this request before and while I had some excellent script books back in my office, I didn't have anything with me at this get-together and in 2005, Google wasn't quite as omnipresent as an adjunct for my brain as it is now. I had yet to learn any fancy Neuro Linguistic Programming techniques for phobia release. I realized I was completely dependent on the words in a script to affect change. I wouldn't admit to my family that I lacked experience, so I said, "Oh, sure, I do that all the time." But when my feet were put to the fire, all I knew how to do for Joe was to hypnotize him to a nice relaxed place and I added what I could remember of the Hartland Ego-Strengthening script and emerged him.

After our impromptu session, Joe acted a little "woozy" and said he was excited to find out "if it worked." My friends and family had many questions for him but at that point all Joe could say was that he certainly felt relaxed. After he moved to Minneapolis, Joe reported back that he was definitely sleeping better however he was still scared of going over bridges. That didn't much change my family's estimation of hypnosis being a bunch of hooey!

More importantly for me, I was not satisfied and wanted additional training. I didn't like being in that place where I did the best I could with the information I had, but it was insufficient to facilitate a change. I demand more of myself – and for my clients. I found the NLP Fast Phobia Cure and that technique enriched my toolkit, yet there was still something missing. I needed to know how to tie everything together and create strong direct or indirect suggestions that last.

You would consider yourself a better hypnotist if you had the secret to creating change without the need of a script, would you not? Well, you are in the right place, because I'm here to share my "secrets" to do just that. Imagine how you will look and feel more confident as you allow the words to come tripping off your tongue automatically. And imagine how comfortable you'll feel with your new ability as you learn to do it easily and quickly.

Some people have the limiting belief that nothing good comes easy. But you are probably already aware that the easier it is, the more you are likely to use it. The more you practice what you learn, the more automatic it comes to you. And, you can begin to use what you learn immediately.

You've already mastered the hardest part of this secret. You already know how to use words! As the new information is fully revealed in these pages, you will notice where you are already using these magic words and language patterns even without full awareness. Imagine how powerful your sessions can be as you comfortably use magic words and language patterns on purpose for a purpose!

As you find yourself speaking hypnotically (using these words and patterns) in full view of a client or a group, you enhance your stature as an expert adding to your ability as a hypnotist. And as you will see, these words and patterns are applicable to EVERYTHING, not just your client sessions. The more you use them, the more natural it becomes, in every conversation.

In hypnosis, we know that preventing or overcoming resistance is a key factor for success. These magic words slip right by the conscious resistance of the critical factor to bring quick results, just like adding hot water to your favorite tea bag. Or the magic words and language patterns can be incorporated into your vocabulary slowly, one at a time for easy gradual successful progression, like the buds forming on a tree in the spring and continuing to bring new joy with that splash of brilliant color through the seasons. Or, you may choose to incorporate the language patterns you learn here all at once to see how much difference it will make instantly. Whichever way works best for you is the best way to use this method of creating Script-less Hypnosis.

Chapter 2: "SCRIPTNOSIS"

It wasn't long in my hypnosis career before I heard a convention speaker pejoratively refer to hypnotists who use scripts as "Script-notists." I was mildly offended but also enlightened. *You mean there's another way?!* Yet, it wasn't immediately revealed how to do the work without relying on what must be the appropriate words to say and in a particular order.

And let me say it plainly right now loud and clear: I am not knocking scripts! To be sure, there are some beautifully written scripts and/or metaphors that you'll want to commit to memory or have at the ready to use when appropriate to augment your change work. Metaphors (long or short) work wonderfully in the subconscious mind by lighting up neural pathways that enhance awareness, connection, and memory. When you find a good story, metaphor or script, adapt it to your needs. And, as you keep learning, well-written scripts can lay a fabulous foundation as you expand your wings and fly into the freedom of owning your craft. With everything in life, we keep adding to our knowledge base and that is what these words and patterns do.

My first adventure into hypnosis was a classic case of "not knowing what you don't know." I went through my training and then went full steam ahead into buying into a franchise hypnosis business. I thought I completely knew how to hypnotize someone, but needed the guidance of a "business in a box" which, like all franchises, had some strict rules and plenty of fees. A franchise hypnosis business also comes with plenty of scripts.

My partner (my long-time friend and former fellow radio personality, Catherine Johns) and I thought it was going to be easy and great fun to read scripts to clients all day. We knew we could do that. We were radio gals and good at reading scripts! Everything was mapped out for us. There was a script for each week of a lengthy program and all the hypnotist had to do was follow along. We primarily worked in the area of weight loss and smoking cessation, and through heavy advertising immediately had a full schedule with enough clients for five hypnotists. And even though those scripts were in no way tailored for the client in our chair, we still had a better than average success rate. And you discover a lot about the success rate when you see a client every week for a package of 26 or 52 sessions!

Scripts do have success and it makes sense that hypnotists want to use them when you realize the subconscious mind (SCM) has so much to do that it looks for shortcuts wherever it can find them. A script provides a sense of ease and calm for the hypnotist. That really appealed to us as we ventured into this new business.

And there's also the placebo effect that aids success as well. I first learned in Dr. Lissa Rankin's book *Mind Over Medicine* about the phenomenon of getting better just from deciding to do so. Researching spontaneous remission and the placebo effect, Dr. Rankin learned about the incredibly high rate of patients who get better as soon as they call a doctor for an appointment. It turns out, just the asking for help (or deciding to make a change) allows the mind and body to begin to align in a way that is healthy and restorative.

Realize, for hypnosis clients, the intention to make a particular change can be the single most important element to making the change and that might happen before the client ever shows up in your office. Utilize that decision to their best advantage!

While client success in our hypnosis center was impressive, I tend more toward an all or nothing strategy so even an 80 or 90-percent success rate did not spell personal success for me. Even when I was just beginning I knew there had to be more that I could offer. I decided to get more training to find out how to help even the most difficult clients. I studied many great techniques from some of the best instructors on the planet as I learned about age regression (from Roy Hunter and Cal Banyan), Forgiveness Work (from Michelle Beaudry) and Parts Therapy (from Charles Tebbetts via Roy Hunter). I incorporated EFT (Gary Craig) and NLP (Patrick Porter, Richard Bandler, Barbara Stepp) and then, thanks to Dr. William Horton's NLP Mater Practitioner training, I really discovered the magic in the words and language patterns.

Perhaps the word games made an instant impact on me because before I discovered my passion for hypnosis, my radio career prepared me to be very familiar with using only words and voice to connect with people. When a client has their eyes closed and they are in a state of hypnosis, I have only words and voice with which to communicate. And I found the words with the most impact for bypass of the critical factor. Interestingly enough, using these words works whether I'm communicating with clients whose eyes are closed or a client who is wide awake in the pre-talk or on the phone. These words and patterns work just as well with co-workers, bosses, spouses and children too, along with hypnosis clients. And they also work well in emails, social media, and...well...this book. You may have already figured out that I am being very intentional with my word choices.

In just a few pages you'll get a list of the magic words and I highly encourage you to use them on EVERYONE. It's good practice, great fun and you will be delighted with the results. Script-less hypnosis works its own magic in your practice. The time you spend looking for and adapting scripts, or writing or re-arranging or editing scripts in preparation for your client is time you've spent reducing your fee. Clients don't pay you for the prep work. And that's time you can now spend with more clients or creating your own products that will help more people while also making you money. Learning these words and language patterns will be time well spent! And don't worry, I've included some tips for using your voice and body language to add some secret sauce to your successful sessions.

Chapter 3: Problematic Scripts

Scripts, as we know, are popular. Aside from the Dave Elman Induction, the Hartland Ego-Strengthening Script gets the most use of any script I've run across. I've heard it delivered verbatim on hypnosis audio recordings. I often hear bits and pieces of it thrown into live or recorded processes.

The Hartland Ego-Strengthening Script in its original form is problematic because it's wordy and very authoritarian which may not be congruent with a more permissive approach. It contains no personal suggestions for your particular client. And unless you understand the rhythm and inflection of the original piece, this script may have your client wincing because of the loss of rapport. The Hartland Script has certainly been updated as times have changed, but the version you will likely see most in books and online is the original with its accompanying limitations. Understand, it is an excellent foundation piece from which to make updates.

My friend and successful hypnotist Jason Linett has adapted it to use the concept as an emerging technique and even as an all-positive piece of hypnotic patter, which he credits to inspiration from fellow hypnotists Lisa Halpin and Ron Eslinger. I've included both of Jason's versions in the Bonus Material at the back of this book in case you haven't seen them before because the gist of the information is excellent to have in your wheelhouse. These scripts are great examples of using the idea in a script, story, metaphor, quote, etc. for versatile patter that can be adapted to a variety of uses. And this all-positive version, in my opinion, is much better than the original.

Certainly you can find a few other good all-purpose scripts to have in your memory for patter purposes. But it may be even better to have a few good metaphors to drop in for understanding. Metaphors are mind magic because they lower resistance to suggestions they contain because the moral of the story makes its own suggestion. Research shows we speak as many as six metaphors a minute as we're communicating our thoughts to others. A metaphor doesn't have to be a long story; it can be a word or two. Stories of any length can be excellent for communicating with the subconscious mind.

> *Imagine…you step into Dorothy's red slippers. Click your heels together three times and say, "There's no place like home…there's no place like home…there's no place like home." Now, as you look in the mirror…find your('re) home…notice you've had many life experiences, have you not? And here you are now, comfortable and…at home. You have everything you need right in your own backyard of experience and wisdom to make all the difference for you now.*

The Wizard of Oz is full of metaphorical material you can use in a variety of ways. Another of my favorite 'all-purpose' metaphors is the simple fork in the road. Although he did not invent the metaphor, I learned the idea first from Cal Banyan in his

Universal Script. You've come to a decision point. You can either stay the same or make a change and you're at a fork in the road. On the left is the low road of least resistance. Taking the client down that road is the aversion technique showing the worst side of things. The high road is the one on the right which may be a little more uphill, but it's the road to success. Take the client up that road peppering heavily with benefits. Then bring them back to the fork in the road and invite them to decide. You don't know which road they'll choose, but you can let them know you believe they will take the RIGHT road for a change!

If you prefer a more generative or spiritual approach, you can use that same metaphor and leave it completely non-contextual or open-ended with little or no guidance other than basic direction and the space for the client to do their own internal work.

> *Imagine you come to a fork in the road and each side will take you where you'll be ten years from now. A person can go on a journey of pretend, can they not?*
> *As you walk down one path notice where it takes you.*
> *Now, go down the other and be aware of where it takes you.*
> *I wonder…which path benefits you the most.*
> *Your choice.*
> *Take a deep breath and start walking.*

Recognize that the bottom line is… it's important to tailor your metaphor, script, technique and yes, the upcoming WORDS AND LANGUAGE PATTERNS to the client with whom you are working.

You can get a copy of Cal Banyan's 'foundational application' of the Universal Script and other great metaphors like Tom Nicoli's

26

car metaphor and Roy Hunter's Confusion Induction at www.Hypnosis.org. Also realize that once you know the story, metaphor, or patter you can drop the script and call upon your knowledge whenever it's appropriate in the session whether that's during the phone consultation, pre-talk, during the actual hypnosis process, emerging or the debrief.

I use Cal Banyan's fork in the road metaphor written out in easy script form as one exercise for my budding Hypnosis Certification students. One day a former student, Mary, called to say she'd run into a problem with that script. Mary's smoking cessation client was 72 years old. Mary wondered if it would be a bad thing to do what it says in the script and take the client ten years down or up that road because she might not even live that long. I reminded her to adapt her material to the client in her office! Can you imagine Mary bouncing her hand off of her forehead? That was all the proof she needed to stop clinging to the scripts. She found she could be much more helpful to her client and make the change work much more relevant as she stayed present with her client instead of focusing so much attention on the words of the script.

The problem with being confined to using scripts is…well…being confined. You spend extra time finding the right script while hoping it addresses the right issue. You may spend more time editing the script to make sure it fits the client than the time you actually spend with the client. You may also have a client who walks in and circumvents your entire planning process by telling you they want to work on something completely different in this session or they didn't want to tell you the whole truth over the phone. And then, quite frankly, there are so many issues in our world with so many aspects and variations that it won't be long before you run across a client who has an issue for which no script has been written. It reminds me of the client who had a fear of silver buttons or a different client who wanted to enjoy the taste of fish during the Lenten season. I know great techniques for change...but I know of no scripts for those particular issues.

If you do use scripts, always pre-read them before use. The script books we were given in my franchise business were a collection of transcriptions of sessions the founder had done with actual clients. The theory was that sooner or later in the 6-month or 1-year program, your client's issues would be addressed. (Most often that turned out to be true so an entire practice built on scripts CAN work.) There were specialty scripts for things like insomnia or nail biting. I'll never forget that insomnia script. It's one I hadn't planned on using and hadn't pre-read it before a client needed that very topic. I'm a good cold reader so it wasn't a problem for me. But then I got to the line that read, "And as you take in a deep breath, Mitch, you can let go of all remaining tension...." Fortunately, I saw the name (that should have been deleted from the transcript) before I said it out loud because my client's name was NOT Mitch! As I said, always pre-read your pre-written scripts.

Scripts can be useful and, as you are now aware, I certainly started out reading scripts. It is a perfectly acceptable way to get started. But also understand that part of what a hypnotist must do is monitor the client's trance. You have to be able to watch your client to track their observable signs of trance and to deepen when necessary. As long as your eyes are glued to a script, you are less effective at calibrating your client's progress with the process. Your client is always processing information outside of conscious awareness. They'll do it with their eyes open or closed.

Chapter 4: Computer/Mind Metaphor

The conscious mind and subconscious mind are always working together to navigate the world. The conscious mind is here and now, logical, analytical, and limited. The conscious mind can hold about seven chunks (or less) of information at any one time. Everything else in the processing loop is done underneath or outside of conscious awareness in the vast subconscious mind...or outside of conscious awareness. This research is based on how the brain stores short-term/ working memory and differentiates it from long-term memory. Understand, the mind is not sectioned off quite so neatly. All of the levels of the mind blend and work together with a single intention... to keep you protected, comfortable and happy. One way to look at it is--the conscious mind is the keyboard on your mental computer offering data entry. The subconscious mind is Google--instantly searching everything you've taken in from the beginning of time for you and sorting to provide the best possible appropriate responses and reactions, right now, based on your perceptions at the time of previous experiences. The perceptual experiences form your beliefs and values and at the speed of thought you determine if this is something familiar or if this is something brand new that needs conscious analysis. It's not a perfect processor...but it's quick!

While the subconscious mind is vast, it likes simplicity. It likes to operate on autopilot. Think about your shower routine. What do you wash first? Your hair? Or do you start with your body and then wash your face and hair? Your shower strategy is right for you; it doesn't make any difference which order you choose for the body cleansing process. The interesting thing is, you do it on autopilot. Most likely, you do it in the same order every time. Human nature tends to have us acting in repeat patterns unless we consciously decide to change. Most people take the same route to work every day, that same well-worn path to the grocery store, and while you're noticing that, you can realize you're not paying much conscious attention to driving. Your conscious mind really only participates to let you know when something is different or changing. You are bounced back into consciousness whenever someone cuts you off in traffic. And most likely you tend to have the same response each time.

Back in the 1940's, neuropsychologist Donald Hebb was known for his work in associative learning. You may have heard of Hebb's Law which states: "Neurons that fire together, wire together." That means that everything we experience—our thoughts, physical sensations/feelings and emotions— trigger thousands of neurons which form a network. It makes it automatic to follow established patterns. As an example, a person who smokes may have their habit linked to certain actions such as starting a car (I've had clients who say they light up as soon as they get into their car as if they have a sensor switch that won't turn the ignition unless there's smoke in the car!) or talking on the phone or having a drink right after a meal. At some point, an action was wired/linked to having a cigarette until the neural networks fired together instantly as if they are supposed to work that way. It becomes an automatic program in the brain like spell-check running in the background on your phone or tablet and firing whenever it detects something unfamiliar. Human experience can lead to very interesting pathways worn through the neural network.

The subconscious mind is economical. It will take the shortest route to get to an action. Why run when walking works just fine. No need to stand when sitting is possible. It wants the easiest, shortest route; after all, the subconscious has a lot of programs to keep running so it utilizes this network of neural pathways to travel familiar routes. It searches for and connects memories, values, beliefs, and internal data to create meaning in an instant—at the speed of thought.

That translates into magic with words because your conscious mind is searching for meaning in what you are hearing. Logic and reason keep the main focus on the subject and the action in the sentence. The subconscious mind is processing the nuance as you instantly decode a spoken message and give it meaning. The data entry system is also, of course, providing data on visual input, smell, taste, or kinesthetic signals. But in this book we will focus attention on how the wordplay impacts the meaning of the suggestion.

Communication with yourself and others already naturally comes from a place deeper inside and quicker than your Conscious Awareness. As you begin now to update your language program, open your mind to the possibilities of the gift of a new tool as each and every word and pattern is revealed.

And now create an image or a feeling in your mind of your unlimited success as you free yourself from the need for a script.

Section 2

MAGIC WORDS

Magic

Maj-ik -----noun

1. *The art of producing illusions as entertainment by the use of sleight of hand, deceptive devices, etc.*

2. *The art of producing a desired effect or result through the use of incantation or various other techniques that presumably assure human control of supernatural agencies or the forces of nature.*

Words

Wurd----noun

1. *A unit of language, consisting of one or more spoken sounds or their written representation, that functions as a principal carrier of meaning. Words are usually separated by spaces in writing, and are distinguished phonologically, as by accent, in many languages.*

Chapter 5: Magic Words

Abracadabra

Ab-ruh-kuh-dab-ruh---noun

1. *A mystical word or expression used in incantations, on amulets, etc., as a magical means of warding off misfortune, harm, or illness.*
2. *Any charm or incantation using nonsensical or supposedly magical words.*
3. *Meaningless talk; gibberish; nonsense.*

It would really be something if there was one magic word that could universally persuade people to do your bidding, wouldn't it?! Well, I'll tell you my pick for the absolute most magic word of them all at the end of this section, but truly they ALL work their wonderful magic.

Abracadabra is a magic code word that works pretty well for explanation of the concept. It's a mystical word that you understand completely upon hearing it. That term *abracadabra* is an incantation of nonsensical sounds that take on a specific meaning in the mind without resistance. You consciously understand that it is vague gibberish, and you may just automatically dismiss it as meaningless talk that does not require conscious intervention. And Presto-Change-o, that is exactly how the words we're discussing here will work for you. But we'll use real, simple words that are common in the English language so it's *like* magic in plain sight or "sleight of mouth."

That's the magic word concept. While our conscious mind, which is primarily concerned with logic and reason, is focusing attention on the subject and verb of a sentence to decode and discover meaning, there is a lot of minutia contained in a sentence that gets little attention. The subconscious mind (some refer to this as the unconscious or non-conscious mind) grabs all the nuance of the connecting and descriptive words outside of conscious awareness. So the magic happens as the words are strategically used by the hypnotist to be perceived by the client as rather "meaningless filler words" that dodge objections and slip DISCREETLY into the subconscious mind where they can work their magic without resistance.

Just as a magician draws your attention to a shiny object in his right hand while the left hand is discretely tucking something into his pocket unnoticed, the hypnotist can naturally draw conscious attention to one thing while suggestions are sliding easily into the subconscious mind.

Realize words are just codes or shorthand for the internal pictures, feelings, sounds, emotions, moods, etc. that are in our imagination, our mind. Words are the code used to get thoughts from the inside of your head out into the open so others can participate in your model of the world. Words can set up agreement or dissent or can be completely neutral.

Here, with this book, you are installing an upgrade to your communication center using much of the software you already have, the words you already know. You are discovering new ways of dropping them into conversation or hypnotic patter in an artful fashion that brings your listener(s) into alignment with your suggestions without resistance. When your goal is to suggest, persuade, or motivate, you want as many forces in your corner as you can muster. And words are always at your ready disposal when you know how to use them to your (and your client's) full advantage.

This list of magic words contains simple, regular words. They don't look or sound different or special like abracadabra—but it's their "ordinariness" that allows them to avoid resistance and sneak past the critical factor and secretly work their magic on the subconscious mind outside of critical conscious awareness. These words create meaning on a deeper level as you offer suggestions for change. It works in the same way as seasoning works on food. You can grill a chicken breast and have edible food. But when you add salt, pepper and some thyme, you create a more robust experience with the meal.

And now, let me unveil some words for you to use to create a more robust hypnosis practice.

Chapter 6: The Top 20 Magic Words

1. **Easily**
2. **Naturally**
3. **Automatically**

Softens whatever comes after

4. **Aware**
5. **Realize**(ing)
6. **Experience**(ing)
7. **Notice**(ing)

Whatever you tell them, they will

8. **Expanding**
9. **Beyond**
10. **Unlimited**

Causes subconscious mind (SCM) to focus on space

11. Before		
12. After		Causes SCM to think of
13. Begin	}	time
14. During		
15. Now		

16. **Imagine**:   Sends the SCM into the (right) creative hemisphere.

17. **Don't**:   The SCM rebels with, "Watch me!" Or missed it altogether.

18. **But**:   The mind automatically negates everything before it.

19. **And**:   The mind naturally includes everything after it.

20. **Because**:   Gives a reason. The mind easily believes everything after.

SCM = subconscious mind.

**For a printable copy of the magic words (and upcoming language patterns), go to www.KarenHand.com/Magic-Words

39

Chapter 7: Softening Suggestions

Let's explore now more closely how the words will work for you as you offer suggestions to your clients.

Relax Resistance

Words 1-3--*Easily, Naturally, and Automatically* are like pieces of stage direction. Whatever follows each of those words is softened as the SCM is directed on how to *easily* accept the new information as a reality in the subconscious world of possibilities.

Hypnosis training often spends a great deal of time teaching how to create smart goals and effective outcomes to form direct suggestions, commands, or affirmations. There are certainly plenty of clients available who will take a direct suggestion and act on it. In fact, some clients do much better with direct commands than they do when presented with options. Yet even the directly suggestible somnambulist likes to hear that something will be easy, natural or automatic.

Let's take the client who wants to exercise more than their current level of movement. You can suggest to some people that they "Move More!" and they will process the command into action. When you have a client who already doesn't much want to exercise or they'd be doing it without seeing you for help, they may need a softer nudge into action. In the pre-talk you will discover their motivations for change and benefits of making that change. Add in a few magic words and you might get a suggestion like this:

> "As you desire to move more *now*, you *easily* find new ways to *automatically* take a flight of stairs instead of the elevator. You *naturally* take the far spot in the parking lot and *easily* walk those few extra steps to the store and to work and to play. You discover the fun in *automatically* looking for new ways to move more."

We haven't even added in basic language patterns and yet the patter becomes rhythmic, hypnotic as you *naturally* find new ways of *automatically* sprinkling in that touch of magic for results with less resistance.

Those three words – easy, natural and automatic – are common examples of words that, like sugar, help the medicine go down. They help the subconscious mind imagine the suggestion as something possible to accomplish. You can increase your vocabulary in this vein by using synonyms as well. After listening to the words your client uses in desultory conversation, you can comfortably season your hypnotic patter smoothly and skillfully with such words as:

Effortless	Freely	Comfortably	Certainly
Calmly	Handily	Simply	Regularly
Conveniently	Quickly	Smoothly	Clearly
Efficiently	Steadily	Skillfully	Definitely

Remember the subconscious mind is economical. It behooves you to keep the patter as simple as possible. You may even think of it as making suggestions to a child. That inner child we hear so much about is the subconscious mind that's always working to our benefit, but sometimes from the perspective of a 3-year old. Simple is effective.

The more you listen to your client's language, the more you'll know which words to use specifically for them. Sometimes a client will smoothly resonate with some words better than others. Use the ones that offer the least resistance to your client's model of the world. You'll know that as you get to know your client. If it is important to them to be smart, use "smarter" synonyms. If you're making suggestions to an accountant, words like efficient and steady might be good choices for softening suggestions in "their" language. A tradesman might like things done skillfully. Realize the magic works just as well as you analyze it less and use the first three words on the list to go ahead and get started now.

Chapter 8: Direct Suggestion

Words 4-7—*Aware, Realize, Experience, Notice* focus subconscious attention so that whatever you suggest for a client to do, they will simply do it. As an example, you might induce a trance by setting up a "yes set" of agreement.

> "You can *notice* now your feet touching the ground…and be *aware* of your hands on your lap…as you *realize* every exhale takes you deeper. Understand you can *naturally* go as deep as you need to go to…*experience* this mind opening trance-formation today."

Notice how the words efficiently guide your client into acceptance. As they do *notice* their feet on the floor (or wherever their feet actually are!) and then *become aware* of their hands, etc. they are in agreement with you or in a "yes set". The more they can say 'yes' with you, the better the rapport and the deeper the trance. As we get into language patterns, you'll learn more about how the direct suggestions are embedded into the patter to sound less like a demand and more like a possibility!

As you experience the simplicity of the wordplay, you understand how beneficial these words will be in your client sessions, pre-talk, group presentations, and other forms of communication.

Additional words that focus attention include:

Observe	Consider	Grasp
Heed	Regard	Envision
Know	Recognize	Think
Understand	Visualize	Accept
Note	Sense	

Understand your words have the power to guide but realize power comes from the acceptance of the suggestion. When there is resistance from your listener, you are likely to be less successful at communicating your message. Imagine the unlimited power you can have when your words guide your client into hypnotic agreement because of your skillful use of the word strategy.

Chapter 9: Go Beyond Limited Beliefs

Words 8-10—*Expand, Beyond, Unlimited* cause the subconscious mind to focus on space. You've been hired by your client to take them beyond their limited beliefs so that instead of remaining the same, they expand their mind/thinking until they have the possibilities of unlimited skills to make the desired change.

I had a client who said she just couldn't motivate herself to do long stretches of hard sweaty exercise. Jillian wanted to get some movement into her life, but she hated the gym finding it depressing to see how fit and agile everyone else was while she felt she would never be able to get in shape. Notice the use of the language—and the magic words as the hypnotic patter might go something like this…

> "As you discover many new ways to move *beyond* the limits of *before*, you now find yourself *easily* taking more steps today than you took yesterday…making the only fair comparison which is between the you of today and the you of

yesterday. You *notice* an extra few steps every day becomes so *simple*. Can you imagine yourself feeling fitter as you *expand* your possibilities now? Taking stairs instead of the elevator for at least a floor or two and looking forward to more and more. Standing and stretching and moving your body between every phone call. And *notice* that as you go looking for opportunities to move more, you find yourself sneaking in more opportunities to move and stretch…and *expand* your options to *easily* find ways of *creating* even more movement. *Realize*, your options *become unlimited* in what you can find to do. And you *magnify* the reality that doing a little bit of something is better than doing a whole lot of nothing…so you *naturally* move more every day."

Of course, you are probably already aware that you don't have to double down on all the magic words in one paragraph or one session. Realize you can easily expand your use of magic words until they are liberally sprinkled throughout your entire process.

These words (and language patterns that you will incorporate soon) can be spread throughout existing scripts or suggestion ideas. When you know your client's goals, and the steps they agree to take to reach the goal plus the benefits they will see, feel, hear, taste and/or smell, you can easily mix and match to generate effective suggestions.

A light trance state is all that is necessary for most habit change such as weight loss, smoking cessation and stress relief. That can be as simple as having a listener's full attention as you speak. You can spend as little or as much time on the induction as you wish depending on your style and whether or not you naturally use rapid, instant, or conversational techniques. A long induction and deepening leaves less time for the therapy, but realize that the words and patterns will be used both while talking with clients wide awake in the pre-talk as well as in the induction, deepening, intervention, post hypnotic suggestions and emerging techniques that you use. And of course, the words and patterns can be used with friends, family, co-workers, and bosses when you find yourself wanting to influence someone to follow your ideas/suggestions.

Additional space-oriented words include but are not limited to:

Elaborate	Embellish	Enlarge	Grow	Increase
Magnify	Open	Unfold	Widen	Boundless
Endless	Full	Full-out	Indefinite	Infinite
Limitless	Unbounded	Vast	Wide	Open
Farther	Extend	Unconditional		

Chapter 10: Time Travel

Words 11-15—*Before, After, Begin, During,* and *Now* trigger the subconscious mind to think of time. You can cleverly direct your client to think of the time you prefer.

These words go fairly unnoticed in desultory conversation, but after you start using these magic words regularly, you'll find it easier, more fun, and automatic to continue to use the magic whenever you communicate. At some point during the fun of the word game, you become aware that you have expanded your skill set as you experience the fluid use and the effectiveness of magic words when you share ideas or make suggestions.

The following example can be used for a smoking cessation client who wants to "taper off slowly" and agrees to make their car a non-smoking environment. Understand this suggestion can also be used for someone who wants to stop eating in the car. And you may find many interesting ways to use this type of patter.

> "You have decided to *naturally* release an unnecessary part of your drive to and from work...or any location for that matter. You have

already experienced how *easy* it is to create a habit while driving. Imagine how *skillful* you already are at creating a healthy habit for good. *Now, before* taking any drive, you *automatically* stash any habitual material...open or closed...in the trunk of your car. *Realizing* that out of sight is out of mind. Not because I say so, *but because* it is your decision. *And during* a drive, you find yourself *noticing* your comfortable breathing...you have many relaxation techniques or games to keep yourself comfortable even *after* you leave the car and move on to other activities."

So travel through time with me for a moment. Before learning something new, we start at the level of unconscious incompetence. We don't even know there is something we don't know...we don't know what we don't know. During the movement through a learning project, the next natural step is conscious incompetence. We suddenly know there is something we don't know and clearly understand that we don't get it...yet.

Step into the way back machine and be at the time when you first learned to drive. There is a lot of expertise you didn't even realize was involved in driving a car. There is steering and putting just the right amount of pressure on the gas pedal for the proper speed or just the right pressure on the brake pedal for stopping in time; checking the rear view mirror and the side mirrors and the speedometer; signaling for turning and changing lanes; and how much space is required to safely move into another lane, etc.

After the first experience behind the wheel, you realize there is a lot to keep track of for the driver-in-training. The student becomes pretty clear/conscious about how much is left to learn and process. (You may be about at that point in discovering word magic now). But be aware that, in just a few days or weeks after driver-training, you are completely alone and driving a car down the street. During that first trip or the first week or month, there is a lot of conscious competence going on. A new driver tends to expend a lot of conscious energy keeping track of all the responsibilities behind the wheel…but it gets easier…and more natural…and much more automatic until now when you drive, and talk on the phone and listen to the radio and have a vivid imaginary conversation with someone in your mind…you are driving without paying much conscious attention at all. Before you even knew it, you reached unconscious competence behind the wheel of a 5-ton vehicle! If you can manage that, you can manage this!!

The learning curve starts with unconscious incompetence, then moves to conscious incompetence, when we realize there is a lot still to learn. Sooner or later your skill level moves into conscious competence, like those early days behind the wheel. The more you practice, the more unconscious competence will occur for you. The more you use it, the more natural and automatic it comes to you!

Additional words drawing attention to time:

Ahead	Formerly	Past
Previously	Behind	Later
Next	Introduce	Trigger
Undertake	Amid	When
Meanwhile	Directly	As
Throughout	Promptly	Until
Back	Forward	Today
Since	Subsequently	Instantly
Induce	Immediately	Future
Momentarily	Prepare	Soon

NOW!

It doesn't matter if you use age regression or timeline insight techniques or whether you prefer guided visualization, meditation, or you use NLP, the words are easily and naturally incorporated for added success in your chosen specialty.

As you review the list of magic words you will notice some words include the possibility of an "ing" ending. That is an added stroke of magic. Take a minute to actually do this upcoming activity now...

Just pause for moment and *experience* the feeling of sitting in a chair (or wherever you happen to be). *Notice* how the word *experience* directs your mind to the specific action. As you have this experience, be curious about how well that word decodes or defines what to do.

Now, as you are *experiencing* the feeling of sitting in the chair while moving through this word play…begin *now realizing* the difference when adding the "ing". That magic 'ing' ending on a word makes it less static; gives it movement.

You can have an *experience*. Or you can *begin now realizing* how it feels different when you are in the trance of *experiencing* it. *Be aware* that it's a subtle shift from single focus to a flow of thought as you are *being aware* of slight shifts in perception.

Chapter 11: Instant One-Word Induction

Word 16 - *Imagine* is a word that sends the subconscious mind into the right, creative hemisphere. Imagine it's a successful day in your office and you realize that you automatically know what to say with each and every client who walks in on this day. Each client is so happy with their change it feels like magic! (Now…come on, you're a hypnotist, actually take a moment to IMAGINE that successful day.)

The word imagine is easily understood by the conscious mind as a right-brain, creative possibility. There's little threat to the logical mind because imagination doesn't have to be logical. Imagination is a game that was played Once Upon a Time (another magical word grouping that naturally sends the mind into the territory of the imagination). The word 'imagine' easily bypasses the critical and judgmental parts of our protective logical and reasonable conscious mind by giving us tacit permission to play outside of boundaries and color outside the lines.

This word works just as well when the eyes are wide open or when closed in a hypnotic trance. In the pre-talk, this word can be used to elicit benefits from your client, "Imagine what life will be like when you have (made the desired change)." In trance, this pro-gression is a wonderful way to help the client rehearse their change by imagining when they will use this insight in their future. As the client vividly imagines several different times or places in their future when they can use the newly discovered skill, they are practicing success. And because the imagination is unlimited, experiencing something in trance can be compared to uploading a new program into a computer/brain; once installed, it's as if it happened in reality and new patterns of thinking are formed.

> "Remember a time when you feel great and have complete confidence in something you are doing (wait for recognition) ...*notice* how you're standing...breathing...be *aware* of the look on your face...*begin* to discover that confident feeling in your body *now* and *expand* your *awareness* to imagine...or even pretend...for a moment that you have that confidence already and notice how that event is different now.
>
> *Imagine* this body posture, this successful look on your face, this feeling of confidence and *extend* it out to the very next time you need it the most..."

Hypnotists might be compared to an up-to-date human GPS. The goal is to get your client to the destination they have chosen. You are, by whatever means available to you, guiding the client along the most efficient route. Just as drivers occasionally veer off of the suggestions given by their friendly GPS voice, clients can stray from your suggestions. It is always a good idea to check in with them to make sure they, and you, are still on track. It is far easier to calibrate your client's response if you can keep a close eye or ear on them (instead of a script) to monitor observable changes.

Before a first formal hypnosis session I tell my clients that I am their guide, but they too have control. Their thoughts are still private, and I do not have a satellite system to read their mind. So, if I suggest they imagine a safe, comfortable place and they start thinking about rush hour traffic, well, we aren't going to the same place and they need to tell me so I can recalculate. That's also valuable feedback...not criticism of your technique. It's feedback to simply recalculate and keep going. The first GPS system I owned had a voice that seemed to me to have an attitude about having to recalculate which increased my stress about arriving to my destination. But she did recalculate every time until we reached the destination 'on the right'. Also useful feedback because I never want my clients to feel as if they've failed or disappointed me which could happen with an impatient tone in my voice. The GPS in my new car is much improved. She PATIENTLY recalculates every time we disagree on a direction...and her patience keeps me feeling secure.

I also let my clients know they can always move or stretch or talk or ask a question and it won't interrupt the hypnotic trance at all. Realize, trance is not as fragile as some might lead you to believe. I have hypnotized people in noisy airport terminals and alongside construction zones. You can suggest, if you choose, to allow every outside noise to help them go deeper or you can just trust that their focused attention is on your voice and their own thoughts and changes. There's a better than average chance that the client in trance will be unaware of any noises or events outside of their trance state.

My first office was on the 6th floor of a medical building on the corner of a busy Chicago intersection. Franchise owner and hypnotist Patrick Porter came to check out the new location and while in town he did a hypnosis demonstration in my office. I got to sit in the recliner and enjoy the experience. We used a lot of hypnotic paraphernalia in that business, hypnotic light and sound machine glasses, headphones to hear voice and music, and CD recorders as all processes were recorded and given to the client. I was suited up and fully participating in the trance led by Patrick's voice in the headphones doing a relaxing process. Observers in the room became quite concerned with audible sirens from passing firetrucks and an ambulance. After the process was finished, I was quizzed about the noise and interestingly enough, I had no idea there was sound other than that of Patrick's voice. It gave me an early experience of how focused a client in hypnosis can be on the voice and words of the hypnotist. I have since learned that is true even when the client has no paraphernalia such as flashing glasses, noise cancelling headphones or soothing music in the background.

Additional words for Imagine:

Envision	Create	Pretend
Conceptualize	Conjure	Fantasize
Invent	Picture	Visualize.

Chapter 12: 2-Step Hallucination

Word 17 - *Don't* think of a dancing pink elephant. Don't think of that pink elephant and whatever you do, don't put purple polka dots on it.

What are you thinking about?

Exactly! It's inevitable that your internal/subconscious processing has to create the picture of the pink elephant with purple polka dots before it can cancel out the picture or thought to follow the suggestion of "don't."

Some say the subconscious mind can't or doesn't or won't process negatives, but that's not entirely true. A negative simply creates an extra step, a two-step process. First we have to imagine (positively hallucinate) the suggestion/the elephant and then (now that it's in our mind) we have to cancel out the picture we just created (negative hallucination). It's easy enough to do in the imagination of the subconscious mind, but it is a two-step process. And if you studied the Harry Arons Depth Testing Scale, you know his claim that one must be pretty deeply entranced (level 5 or 6) to have positive or negative hallucinations. (Now, that was easy wasn't it? And you managed that depth level while reading a book!)

There are little kids all over the world sitting in a time out right now because their mother said, "Don't slam the door on the way out." And later when the child went outside, as soon as the door slammed, he or she slapped their forehead and said "Oh, that's what I wasn't supposed to do!"

Ironically, Mom could have controlled the entire situation simply by saying, "Go out of the door quietly." Or better yet, "Imagine going out the door quietly." Kids of all ages can conjure up many ways to exit a door quietly. One could tip-toe, or hold the door handle carefully until completely closed, or even leave the door open; at least it didn't slam!

With the word don't, there is also a chance for resistance if the client starts thinking something like "Don't tell me what to do!" Interestingly, that can be turned into a wonderful positive for a hypnotist to use on purpose in a session. "Don't relax too quickly because you can easily relax now at your own comfortable pace." Or "Don't go into trance now..." There is a definite presupposition that the trance will occur and the subconscious mind simply decides when by internally responding, "Watch me go into trance as quickly as I want to!" or "I won't go yet, but I will in a moment." Either way the client goes into a nice hypnotic state of heightened suggestibility/receptivity.

If you are giving direct suggestions, it can be a good idea to simply avoid the word don't. But imagine how many ways you can make use of the 2-step thinking process to guide your clients into a hypnotic trance state. You might even fantasize about having friends or relatives follow your every word as you suggest, "You don't have to believe only me, because experts worldwide agree that it's true." (Not just yet, but in a moment, we'll discuss my favorite magic word and, when we do…remember…don't smile as you find yourself thinking of this particular example because it works!)

You may choose to use the "don't" word creatively or leave it out altogether. Either way is better.

Chapter 13: Now You See It...Now It's Gone!

Word 18 - *But* is a tiny yet powerful word. It's the master at making things disappear. But is an interesting word because once uttered, the mind erases everything that came before it in a sentence or a thought...poof...just like magic.

Growing up as an only child, I liked elementary school because it provided plenty of people to talk with and I liked to talk! And, I guess because of being an only child, my mother saved everything I ever did. That gave me an opportunity to look back on some elementary school report cards and it amazed me to see how some of my teachers unwittingly got me into trouble. More than once on report cards in several grade levels, teachers had written, "Karen is a good student, but she talks too much."

Please take a moment to notice the first part of that sentence and, like me, maybe you'll wonder why I was not praised for being a good student. I was however scolded several times for being such a talker because of that heat-seeking B-U-T missile. It canceled out any praise of my abilities as a student and simply focused my mother's attention on the "less than perfect" aspect of my propensity for verbal communication. What no one seemed to understand at the time was that it was the fact that I had people with whom to talk that made school so interesting for me! Take that away and my performance as a student might have dropped off significantly.

Notice the use of the connecting word "but" and realize that it cancels out whatever is said before it in the sentence. "You are doing very well, but relax even deeper now." In that context, a hypnotist is guiding the client into relaxation through praising their effort...which is unfortunately immediately cancelled out as the client hears "*but you need to do more to completely relax.*" If one is actually telling the client to do more, that's an appropriate use. If the hypnotist is wanting to stack the suggestions so the client will do even more of that...then leave out the "but."

You can use the but word positively in this way:

> "You may drift off and have a variety of thoughts *but* your subconscious mind continues to go deeper with the sound of my voice."

> "You may hear every word I say or you may drift off and think about something else entirely *but realize* you continue to become more relaxed with every exhale."

> "I could suggest tension in your body--relaxation is not really necessary for hypnosis, *but* you find

yourself *becoming* so comfortable now, it is *easy* as you relax completely."

You are probably already aware that guiding a client into that altered state called hypnosis is a process of giving a few simple directions and allowing the client to follow those suggestions. The more they comply, the more deeply they go into hypnosis. Compound the suggestion with an experience and the result deepens again. So, the more you give suggestions that are real for the client, the more they trust you and the process. But you can instantly pop the client out of hypnosis if you give a suggestion that is rejected by the client's beliefs or values. Understand the power of the word and use it to the client's advantage.

And there are other words that have a similar impact:

However	Although	Nevertheless
Still	Though	Yet

Chapter 14: The Amazing Multiplier

Word 19 - *And* is a secret suggestion to the mind to automatically include everything that follows it. When you want to increase a feeling and enhance a state and deepen the trance, you can string your suggestions together with that 3-letter plus sign, the magic word "and."

This little word adds rhythm to your hypnotic patter and allows the mind to naturally go along with a suggestion and helps to meander your client into complete acceptance of your suggestions. It may not be grammatically correct but it works! You may even be aware now that the writing of this book is often using more hypnotic language than actual grammatically correct rules. It's interesting to me because I'm even in a Facebook group called GASP, Grammar and Spelling Police. I do know the rules! And typically, I'm a stickler! My editor, Kelly Epperson, could be a card-carrying member of that group. She questioned the formation of some sentences and the use of that "and" word and the use of "…". But she's a quick study and has been able to comfortably join the rhythm of the patter and let the hypnotic language progress. She's even intrigued by the movement provided in an "ing" ending. Yet, she still prefers the more direct standard language of the page.

The good news if you're just learning the strategic use of these words (and upcoming language patterns) is that when you use them enough, they become a standard part of your everyday language when you want to persuade, motivate, or coach.

And now, back to the word "and." For a particularly analytical client, Nan, who rejected direct suggestions but did very well with options, I helped her increase her exercise time each day with patter something like this:

> "I don't know if you will *automatically* take the stairs instead of the elevator at work...*and naturally* park farther away from the store when you go shopping...*and* find a ladies' room on a different floor at your office to sneak in extra steps...you may *also* choose to join a gym *and* hire a personal trainer...I don't know exactly how but you will find the best options to move more...*and* you find yourself looking for every opportunity *now* to *experience* more movement in your daily routine."

Several suggestions are included in the patter based on ideas we discussed before the hypnosis session began. The pre-talk guided Nan into problem solving and she came up with solutions that had already started germinating in her mind. The hypnotic trance allowed her to fully imagine taking action for more exercise without conscious resistance. As Nan imagines the change taking place, she is already rehearsing her success.

64

Manifesting, a concept often discussed in hypnosis circles, is an "and" proposition. It begins with a thought then expands into benefits. You can see how this works, can you not? As I considered the idea of learning hypnosis skills, I wondered what I might do with the skill set and began to consider using it with friends, and then clients, and I imagined a Hypnosis Center with several working offices. And the more I thought about it, the more I imagined the fun my business partner and I would be having in such a lovely center, and sharing a manager's office where we can talk and laugh and go to lunch every day planning our strategy for having the best hypnosis center in Chicago! It was indeed a beautiful fantasy. The more I envisioned our center, the more steps I took to make it a reality. And the more I built up the benefits, the closer I got. And, yes, we were awarded Center of the Year throughout the franchise in our first year in business.

That fantasy manifested into a reality - except for the daily lunching out! We quickly had a full enough schedule that we staggered our hours. Catherine opened the office at 9am and I came in later and closed at 9pm. We weren't able to "lunch for fun." Then my mother's failing health demanded my full-time attention in 2011. That's when we decided to close the physical facility. I continued to see clients in my home office and when I returned to full-time practice my business expanded beyond the limits of home. I do a great deal of remote training and workshops and speak at a variety of conferences. Catherine followed her calling to become a speaker's coach. You can read exceptional tips in her book *Show Up and Shine* which she manifested by considering all the "additional" opportunities that could bring to her coaching business. And now we're able to lunch for fun because we still need that time to get together to laugh.

Imagine how you will be able to help your clients achieve their goals as you stack desires and benefits and practice success in the hypnosis session building up a strong enough desire that the subconscious mind takes over to work out the details. And imagine your own thriving lucrative successful practice!

Additional AND words for variety:
        Also   Plus   Including   Additionally.

Chapter 15: Because, It's Magic

And now, a drum roll, please!

BECAUSE ... it works!

Word 20 *BECAUSE* This is my favorite (and maybe THE most powerful) magic word of them all because there is a natural and automatic tendency to easily accept everything that comes after this word without judgement or resistance.

One of my favorite pieces of research ever is a 1977 Harvard study in human behavior published in the Journal of Personality and Social Psychology, way back in ancient times before people had personal computers at home much less on their wrist or their cell phone. It was a time when Harvard students had access to only one photocopying machine in the student library and often there was a line of people waiting for their turn to make copies.

Psychologist Ellen Langer gave her research assistants specific instructions to conduct a study on human nature. They used that long line at the library copy machine for their lab.

It was a clinical study, so there were three "control" tests. In the first version, the research assistants made a request of people in the copy machine line using only these words, "Excuse me, I have 5 pages. May I use the Xerox machine?" Those students must have been pretty good-natured and patient there at Harvard back in the late '70s because 60% of the people in line let the assistant cut in with that request.

In the second version, the assistants gave a real reason for needing the special treatment, "Excuse me. I have 5 pages. May I use the Xerox machine, because I'm in a rush." Interestingly, just adding the reason increased the cut rate to 94-percent of the requests. It makes sense because the conscious mind wants a reason/answer for everything and tends to accept it when there is an explanation.

But now comes the most amazing part of the study. In Version 3, the assistants had a fake reason and said, "Excuse me, I have 5 pages. May I use the Xerox Machine, because I have to make copies?"

You and I both know every student in that copy machine line was there because they had to make copies. And yet, using the word *because*, even with a silly fake reason following it, still allowed for a 93-percent success rate in cutting in line!

The success wasn't in the reason; it was in that tiny critical-factor-eluding word BECAUSE!

The conscious mind is the great naysayer. The protective purpose of this part of our mind is that it uses logic and reason to filter the information going into the imaginative subconscious mind. The SCM has unlimited ability to create and yet it doesn't distinguish between fact and fiction, real or pretend. In the subconscious mind, all things are possible. As hypnotists, we want to play in the realm of possibilities and solutions. So we use whatever is necessary to bypass the much ballyhooed critical factor-- AKA the "yeah-but" factor. "Yeah, but (this) or yeah, but (that)."

The critical factor is a fine line between conscious logic and reason and subconscious imagination. There are many ways to cross that critical factor. You may have learned about instant/rapid inductions or "shock" inductions. These provide a moment of time when the mind is completely open to a solution and a suggestion can easily slip right into the imagination. There are progressive inductions where you relax the mind so much that it just wants to go along. There are confusion inductions that can get through the thick armor of the most analytical client. And then there are these word games. The word games have the magical power of warding off criticism or judgement and sliding right into the world of possibilities without resistance. It's based on human nature and how the mind processes information.

That critical factor evolved to protect each individual version of the reality we've created in consciousness from being too easily threatened. It makes snap judgements about how incoming information compares to what we already believe. Information that lines up with our established beliefs is granted automatic admission and information that goes against our value system is denied entrance. (And, yes, denied even in trance). Unless that information/suggestion finds a crack in the armor or a back door or an open window.

And that's where the words have a chance to work their magic. They slither right through the tiniest crack because they have a secret power...the cloak of invisibility. So common, they go unnoticed. You could say they're hiding in plain sight and work like magic by doing the trick while your conscious mind is focused over here on the subject and action of the sentence.

The conscious mind is all here and now analytical thinking. The critical factor is looking for similar thinking which is satisfied right there in the conscious mind because you're giving a reason for the request. No criticism or judgement, we've got our reason, send that request or suggestion right on in to the subconscious mind to start creating solutions. In the case of the copy machine line, the conscious mind said "Sure, go ahead of me, and make your copies!" Only 7% of the people in the research study resisted the suggestion when the word "because" was used.

> *Imagine* what can happen as you find yourself *automatically* using magic words to help your clients *easily* reach their goals *now because* that's what they want *and because* that's why they're paying you. You can *imagine adding* these words *comfortably* into your patter to *create* a set of suggestions, can you not?

Realize, this is a skill your client already performs very well. After all, a client who now wants to release the habit of smoking has been smoking up to now because they've been giving themselves a reason to do it. I'm guessing their reason to inhale a carcinogen into their lungs wasn't very sound because well, it couldn't have been, could it? And now because your clients know how to turn a reason into action, it's simple for you to help them transition their new reason because it's what they want.

Sooner or later you will notice the rhythm, and be aware of the elegance, and understand that it is simply a matter of spicing up the client's benefits with words that allow the suggestion for change to flow unhindered into the world of possibilities. Let these magic words do their magic for your clients and for your practice!

Section 3

Hypnotic Language Patterns

Chapter 16: Hypnotic Patterns

"Imagine no possessions. I wonder if you can."
~John Lennon

You are probably already aware that I have been using not only magic words but exciting language patterns throughout the writing of this book. The words and patterns work effectively in vocal communication, and also can be used in a variety of ways in print and social media. You may have already noticed that internet marketers use hypnotic language and strategies in their sales material. After a workshop I did on Magic Words and Language Patterns one attendee commented to another on the way out, "I don't know if this is the best workshop I've ever attended…or if she hypnotized me to believe that." I wonder if both are true?

Without fancy inductions or confusion techniques, the language patterns are a conversational means for creating a hypnotic trance state for even the most analytical clients because they don't sound like a suggestion or command. The conscious mind puts up less

74

resistance while the fertile subconscious mind is being seeded with transformative ideas. Once a client is deeply in the trance state, you can easily move into more simple, direct language because you've already bypassed the resistance.

Remember, a trance state is not a flat line. (Thank goodness!) It's much more like a wave. You can think of it perhaps as a span of attention. That state you go into every night right between being wide awake and being sound asleep, that's a light hypnoidal stage called the hypnogogic state. When you go from fast asleep to wide awake, that's got a long and fancy name too, called the hypnopompic state. All day as you drift in and out of conscious awareness, you're moving seamlessly from trance state to trance state, at times deeper and at times in a lighter state of trance. The moment you realize you are day-dreaming; you've just emerged yourself from a nice hypnotic state. When you pull up in front of your house and realize you don't remember anything at all about how you got there, you've just effortlessly emerged yourself from "Highway Hypnosis." It's that simple and that's how easily our trance states automatically occur every day.

In fact, when you do a deep dive into consciousness and altered states, you realize we're in a form of altered state all the time unless we are completely conscious. When you have lunch with your girlfriends, you're in the girlfriend trance. When you go home to the family, you comfortably move into the family trance. You're probably already very familiar with the work trance, the traffic trance, the parent trance, the TV trance…etc. It's as if we flip the switch to auto-pilot. As I write these words, I find myself happily involved in the book-writing trance.

So whether you're in a conversation or deeply spellbound in an altered state of mind, unless you are drugged/anesthetized or knocked out, you are drifting in and out of levels of conscious awareness. A trance state is the easy part! It's staying connected to the here and now or full consciousness that's hard to maintain.

Can you imagine now how easy it will be to en-trance your clients during the pre-talk? And through the process of fractionation, you are probably already aware that each time a person goes into a little trance and comes out, the next trance will be easier and deeper. Sooner or later you'll completely enjoy the various ways you have of creating trance and change with your clients. And it is beginning to really get exciting, isn't it, because you've learned so much already.

Using these language patterns, you discover the magic in a turn of phrase. And you understand the elegance of figuratively installing new mind software without hesitation or resistance. You can already begin to appreciate how these natural patterns increase your skills, can you not? And as you find yourself free from the grip of the scripted words on a page, you naturally devote more attention to being with your client. And if you practice frequently, then you will improve rapidly. Now, try to resist practicing these skills on everyone you meet! Sooner or later you will fully acknowledge how easy the patterns are to remember and use and how successful your suggestions become.

The previous paragraph is chock-full of language patterns and embedded suggestions (sometimes called embedded commands or indirect suggestions) which are simply suggestions delivered conversationally to decrease resistance. Your suggestions/ideas/motivational thoughts can comfortably be delivered in conversation, in person or on the phone, to your friends and family or to your dry cleaner. In other words, you can use this information in any communication to increase the results of the communication. And you will notice how quickly the skill set goes easily tripping off the tongue when used in a deep trance state as well. Add the strategic use of words and language patterns to your client's desires linked to their benefits and add in anything else that you already know (or learn) how to do (such as metaphor or stories or regression or parts work) and the more you practice the skillful use of language, the more successful your various techniques and your practice becomes. It seems to work...like magic!

There are hundreds of lyrical language patterns, each expertly directing attention to an intended outcome. And each contains a direct suggestion couched in gentle language. It is possible that these language patterns can be used universally on both directly and indirectly suggestible people. It could be that these so-called "sleight of mouth" techniques will work on most of the people most of the time and it could be that a truly directly suggestible person will simply hear just the direct suggestions embedded in the patterns anyway.

My uncle, Frank, enjoyed telling a story about his church. For several months the priest and church parishioners had been hearing a knock in the pipes. They called out a variety of tradesmen to determine what was causing the noise and all had no answer. They were about ready to call an exorcist when a parishioner suggested they talk with her dad who'd been a plumber for fifty-two years.

The old plumber and the priest walked through the church and occasionally could hear the noise. After about twenty minutes, the old plumber took a small hammer out of his tool belt and tapped on a pipe three times. The noise stopped. The plumber told the priest he'd check back in a week.

One week later, the pipes were still quiet as a church mouse. The old plumber had fixed the problem and the priest was quite pleased. That is until he got the invoice three days later. The bill was $1,000! Immediately the priest called the plumber to inquire how a 20-minute visit and three tiny taps could be so expensive. The plumber explained that it was only $50 for the taps, but it was $950 for knowing where to tap!

And that's certainly a key to successful hypnosis, whether you use meridian tapping or not. Being present with your client and listening to their answers to determine the best therapeutic technique for the most efficient change work allows you to know where to tap into success and what technique will be most efficient. You can discover more about The Outcome Intervention on my website www.KarenHand.com/Magic-Words. For now, realize you can freely use these patterns along with your current techniques as you observe your clients going quickly and deeply into a trance-formative hypnotic experience.

Chapter 17: Top 10 Language Patterns

1. You probably already know...

2. Can you imagine...

3. You can _____, can you not?

4. A person is able to_____

5. Sooner or later....

6. Try to resist...

7. If you _____, then _____.

8. _____ said _____.

9. What happens when you _____?

10. The more _____, the more _____.

**For a printable copy of the language patterns, go to
www.KarenHand.com/Magic-Words

As you discover the following language patterns, notice that the pattern will be bold, the magic words underlined, and the direct suggestion/embedded command will be italicized for easy identification.

1. You Probably Already Know

> On a deep level, **you probably already know**
> that as you expand your skills, success increases.

I'm not suggesting anything new to you. Any resistance is stopped in its tracks because the conscious mind can automatically presume it to be true since "you probably already know it anyway." Then the embedded suggestion (in this case— expand your skills to increase your success) goes directly into the SCM of possibilities to go looking for evidence of what you already know. Without resistance, you (or your client) can instantly access memories, thoughts, sounds, or pictures of learning something new and having increased success. Experiencing that congruence by remembering something similar in your life compounds the suggestion and deepens the trance.

You may not be consciously aware of this internal automatic program searching for evidence. But you will always get what you're looking for because the mind is a goal-oriented mechanism. And the SCM is a memory bank, a storehouse of everything you've ever experienced, remembered or re-vivified from your perspective at the time of the experience. And your mind is always searching for and getting answers without bothering to take up space in conscious awareness.

If you received a sticker after studying for and passing a spelling test in elementary school, that memory may come to you compounding the suggestion of new skills increase success or bring rewards.

Realize a compounded suggestion is a suggestion that is then experienced thus making the suggestion stronger to last longer. So as you recall that memory it serves as proof and your SCM can easily say, "Yes, I already know how rewarding it can be to learn and use new things." And remember, this processing is happening mostly outside of conscious awareness or critical interference.

> **You probably already know** that *short bursts of exercise throughout the day* work just as <u>efficiently</u> as <u>extended</u> periods in the gym.

> **You are probably already aware** that *hypnosis was approved by the AMA in 1958* as an <u>effective</u> <u>and</u> legitimate modality for change.

> In fact, **you probably already know** that most people who *experience hypnosis* are helped by it.

> So <u>now</u>, **can you imagine** how your *rewards multiply* <u>as</u> *you use this valuable new pattern?*

2.   Can You Imagine...

> **Can you imagine** just how *easily* you are *integrating* these patterns

Most people will readily admit to having an imagination. In this language pattern, I'm not suggesting or demanding anything of you, I'm just curious if you can imagine. And even the protective parts of the conscious mind can effortlessly go down the path you're suggesting. **Can you imagine** interesting new ways to help clients <u>because</u> *you include this pattern in sessions* as you <u>expand</u> your skillset? *You can, can you not!*

Dopamine is one of my favorite organic brain chemicals. It motivates us to set goals and take action toward them because of the surge of pleasure that occurs when we reach our goals. Many brides have experienced that dopamine effect followed by the hangover – from the loss of the dopamine rather than from too much champagne. Amid all of the planning, meetings and fittings, there are often parties and showers and gifts along the way, many ways to experience the rewards of a budding relationship. Dopamine surges as the bride experiences the little rewards along the way and there is a lot of pleasure. The beautiful day arrives and it is everything she wants followed by a lovely honeymoon to start the relationship. The mood is high. And then a week or two after returning from the trip and settling into a new routine of life, the post-event blues can set in.

Neuroscientist Steve Ilardi of Brain Chemistry LifeHacks says you can avoid the letdown by setting a new goal or goals before you've actually slumped after a massive high whether it's a wedding, graduation, or any other project that captivated your attention until completion. (Writing this book comes to mind for me! The new goal? More books!) Go ahead and experience the feeling of the Dopamine effect by setting your goal now to practice these patterns at the first and every opportunity. Feel good and get a good laugh which compounds that good feeling!

People are more likely to do what they are familiar with. So this is a great "session hack" because it doubles the effectiveness as you lower resistance by just wondering if your client can imagine what you're suggesting and as they do imagine it, they are practicing success and becoming more familiar with it. Loop through the process a couple of times and you have repetition driving familiarity.

This pattern smoothly utilizes benefits to making a change:

> **Can you imagine**... *you having so much extra money* <u>because</u> *you release that old habit?* I ***wonder*** what *you'll do for yourself* with that extra cash.

> **Can you imagine** where you *practice these language patterns* <u>*immediately*</u> <u>and</u> <u>*develop*</u> *confidence in your ability?*

> **Can you imagine** you *using this language pattern* to enhance success thinking for yourself <u>and </u>your clients?

> <u>And</u> **you can** <u>begin</u> to grasp <u>now</u> how <u>easily</u> *you put this magic into regular use*, **can you not?**

3. You Can _____, Can You Not?

You can *shift your awareness to your breathing*, **can you not?**

Of course you can! It's a very simple thing to do and asking the question makes the embedded suggestion (shift your attention to your breathing) much less threatening. Plus, using the great statement closer "can you not?" makes it more confusing to help ward off resistance or disagreement.

The conscious mind is very limited in its capacity, holding only about seven chunks or less of information at any time and can focus on only one thing at a time. Decoding the word-symbols or sounds we use for communication becomes a little more complicated to the resistant critical factor when you layer in the word pattern nuances. The rhythm becomes trance-inducing, the words require no effort to process and the suggestions for change are what the client wants. The process all becomes very congruent and easy to follow and accept when you have been present with your client doing a good job of gathering the appropriate information necessary for making a change. You simply plug in the changes the client will accept and the benefits they will reap. And it's all held together with a sprinkling of magic.

You can *appreciate the benefits of committing to regular exercise to reach your goal*, **can you not?** This suggestion, of course, applies to a client who WANTS to commit to regular exercise.

A client who does not have a regular schedule but wants to get as many steps as possible every day may get a series of suggestions something like this:

"You can *choose a variety of ways every day to take more steps,* **can you not? You probably already know** that the latest research shows *short bursts of exercise throughout the day* are just as <u>effective</u> as <u>extended</u> workouts <u>because</u> *the body benefits either way.* **Can you imagine** <u>now</u> *taking the stairs* instead of the elevator, <u>and</u> *parking farther away* at the store <u>and</u> *standing <u>and</u> walking in place <u>after</u>* completing *every phone call at work?* **You can** clearly now *walk a path with opportunities for more daily steps,* **can you not?**
A person is able to *sneak in exercise all day* long <u>and</u> *be surprised at how easy it is to increase the step count.*

I added a fourth language pattern to the end of that patter which I'll explain in just a moment. But that list of suggestions is an example of how to take the client's desired change, more steps…without a routine…and install a new habit or set of behaviors simply by plugging desires and benefits into the language patterns. A client who wants or needs to do more exercise but hasn't yet been able to imagine having the time or inclination to join a gym may now be able to imagine walking the grocery cart all the way back inside the store after each trip. And if they can imagine it, they can do it, and when they do it, they achieve more steps (and compound the suggestion!). Success breeds success and the more steps they take to accomplish their goal, the closer they find themselves achieving what they want.

You may already be aware that the patterns can be used in the pre-talk as you are gathering information. And then the agreed upon actions can be reinforced in the hypnotic state. Suggestions can be installed through compliance and repetition...or through trauma.

Some hypnotists offer recorded suggestions or reinforcement audios. The repetition is an excellent way to maintain the suggestion as long as the client actually listens to the recording. In truth, actually setting aside time to listen is a good buy-in for beginning to make a change. If the client is willing to listen daily, they are definitely showing compliance and a desire for change. If they link their success to listening to an audio recording, they will continue to have success as long as they listen. If the success strategy starts there and then is expanded to actually be linked to the actions they take, they will continue to have success as long as they continue to take action.

I have found that for some clients, taking action is too big a step at first to make it past the "yeah-but" factor. But agreeing to "listen" or "think" their way to change may be doable. In that event, repetition is an ally for change so offer recordings that suggest easy, incremental actions that they are willing to take. Then along the way, as they are taking action, shift their success anchor to their dedication to taking action!

Trauma is another way to install a new behavior. We learn things instantly all the time. My friend, Cathy, is a fast-driving, no-nonsense woman. We used to joke about the true meaning of the color-coding on stop lights. Everyone knows that green is go and red means stop. And Cathy and I firmly agreed that yellow meant speed up to get across the intersection. Cathy lived by that rule until one day she went through the yellow light just one second too late and opposing traffic had proceeded on their green light. Cathy's car was t-boned. Luckily she wasn't hurt, but her car was in the car hospital for a month and a half! That was definitely a traumatic wake-up call. And instantly, she changed her thinking and now slows down and stops for a yellow light. Voila! A traumatic suggestion that changed her behavior and lasts.

Doctors (often unwittingly) have some success with the "trauma" approach to conversational suggestions. "You have a serious throat infection and will have to take this antibiotic to feel better!" That's an example of a "trauma" based suggestion that leads the patient to filling their prescription and taking their medicine, at least until the symptoms go away. The incentive for following the suggestion to take the medication wanes once the sore throat feels better.

Suggestions last as long as there is repetition or as long as the suggestion is useful. In a stage show, if a hypnotist tells a subject to forget his own name after the show is over and then later in the evening calls on him and he can't remember his name, the suggestion remained useful for the show. If there had been a million-dollar give-away before the man's name was restored to memory by the hypnotist, and if the subject's name had been called for the winning ticket, he would no longer have had a use for that suggestion and it most likely would have instantly just gone away. **A person is able to** *make sense of all this*, I am sure!

4. A Person Is Able To _____.

> **A person is able to** *benefit from these suggestions as long as they are useful.*

For most people, when they hear comments on what other people can do, they do their own internal check to see if they can do it too. The internal scan goes mostly unnoticed by the conscious mind. When a hypnotist sets up this comparison and gives a perfectly acceptable and possible suggestion, there is agreement. That deepens the rapport, it deepens the trance and it deepens the suggestion.

There is an added bonus to this pattern in that it dissociates the client temporarily. As the comparison is set in motion, the subconscious mind instantly moves into an observer position and goes running through the past, looking for assurance that it is as capable as the next person. While that occurs the conscious mind waits for a reasonable answer and gets out of the way of the suggestion. Without resistance, the subconscious mind can easily find past examples of doing something similar that produced positive results. It will then generalize examples that enhance the pattern. Realize all of this processing takes milliseconds outside of conscious awareness.

If I were to ask two people to look around a room and count as many blue items as they can find in 30 seconds and then compare the results, as soon as they agreed to enter the game (compliance) their eyes would start darting around to find as many blue items as possible to win the game. The SCM wouldn't be very selective about what qualified as blue. Baby blue would qualify on the same level as royal blue or navy or even blue-green. The mind would generalize to collect as many items as possible. In that same way, when one hears that a person can do something, they're going to scroll through their memory banks to make sure they are just as capable as the next guy.

While all that comparison shopping is being done, the suggestion settles in easily with the first example of agreement. The SCM is efficient. As soon as it arrives at evidence of having the capacity to do it, the suggestion is taken and then it's as good as done.

A person is able to *make the changes she wants,* <u>and</u> *allow them to be permanent.*

A person is able to *discover meaningful changes* <u>simply</u> … <u>because</u> *you want to do it for* yourself.

A person is able to <u>*realize*</u> *the health benefits of being smoke free.*

A person is able to <u>understand</u> that *this word pattern is very powerful* alone or in combination with magic words and other language patterns.

Sooner (or later…) *you improve all of your communication* when *you use magic words and hypnotic language patterns,* <u>now.</u>

5.   Sooner Or Later…

Sooner or later you will *deeply enjoy* just how *naturally* these patterns *flow.*

The sooner or later language pattern rolls off the tongue comfortably because everything happens sooner or later. There is also a strong pre-supposition that the suggestion will happen, the only decision you need to make is whether it happens now or a little later than now. Either way, it will happen.

In a pre-talk with a client who is seeking help for smoking cessation, the theory of provocative therapy would certainly chip away at a limiting belief of not being able to do it, with the comment, "Well, **sooner or later** *everyone quits smoking.* You're here to make sure *you do it while you're still alive!*"

Hypnotists who use aversion therapy are probably already aware of the many uses for this pattern.

> **Sooner or later** *you notice the disgusting taste and smell of a cigarette* before *you decide to keep it away from your mouth.*

> **Sooner or later** you will be offered a tempting treat but your power is in *realizing the importance of comfortably sitting on the floor playing with your grandkids.*

> **Sooner or later** *you discover the unlimited benefits of experiencing hypnosis.*

Sooner or later you <u>become aware</u> that *hypnosis is the <u>efficient</u> way of reaching your goals.*

Sooner or later *you find yourself using this <u>natural</u> language pattern with everyone.*

Try to resist <u>noticing</u> *yourself having fun* as *you use successful word play on your kids or your spouse!*

6. Try To Resist…

Really try to resist *going deeply into trance*

Try is a very interesting word. We use that code often in conversation and mostly without understanding its impact.

One of the most important jobs of a qualified hypnotist is to discover as quickly as possible how the client is thinking about an issue or how they are doing a habit. The only thing we know for sure as we begin working with a client is that the way he or she is currently doing something isn't working to their satisfaction. And, yes, we all know that the definition of insanity is doing the same thing over and over again and expecting a different result. But it's often hard for us to recognize our own insane habits, we call it routine. So, the hypnotist listens to discover how the client is doing a thing because then if the client takes a suggestion to do anything differently there will at least be a different outcome. When that difference is combined with actions the client actually agrees to take, they are on the road to success.

91

When a client says they will try to do something, you can be pretty sure they are not committing to the change. If I were to tell you, "I tried to go through a door," what would you automatically assume? You'd most likely assume I did not make it through the door. Otherwise, I would have said "I went through the door." And when a client says they will try or they did try to do something, you can bet they're lining up excuses already.

In fundamental suggestibility testing, new hypnotists are taught to help a client experience the phenomenon of hypnosis through catalepsy, eye lock or arm catalepsy. To test the effectiveness of a suggestion, there is often an additional suggestion to try something with no results. You'll recognize the familiar Dave Elman command, "Try to open your eyes and you cannot. Try and you cannot. Try and you cannot."

That code word try implies failure. So as you suggest relaxation to your client you could say "Relax from the top of your head all the way down to the bottom of your feet." Or you could suggest, "**Try to resist** the desire to *relax completely now*." The implication is easy to understand as it implies that you will try, but you won't be able to do it. And as the client notices the letting go more and more, their belief in the process gets deeper and the deeper they go into a hypnotic state. You can also use your voice inflection to strengthen this implication.

Hypnosis doesn't have to be so serious. When I first meet with a client, we play a lot of games and have a lot of fun. Laughter is good for our health. And as we get playful with the imagination, the rapport strengthens and helps ensure success. I like to attach magnets on the tips of the clients' fingers and I can tease that the harder they **try to keep their fingers apart,** the stronger the magnetic pull becomes as I watch them try and not be able to with glee! In my experience, 98 percent of clients are amazed that their fingers pull together even when they **try to resist**. It seeds the idea that trying doesn't achieve the result and it helps us both know they can experience hypnosis…because they had their eyes wide open and heard every single word I said and yet there were still imaginary magnets in their fingers! Later in a more formal state of hypnotic trance, I can again suggest that they, "**Try to resist…**" and sometimes I get a smile as the client just enjoys deepening their own trance.

It's a handy phrase as you are persuading groups or prospective clients in a phone consultation and any other communication where you want to have your suggestion or idea be easily accepted.

> **Try to resist** realizing that *hypnosis is effective for positive change*
>
> **Try to resist** believing that *you are worth the effort to eat premium foods and maintain your health.*
>
> And now that *you know the truth about restaurant food,* **try to resist** *noticing the healthiest options first on any menu.*
>
> **Try to resist** *having fun with this pattern* and you cannot!

If you *practice often*, **then** *you will do it effortlessly* very soon.

7. **If You** _____, **Then** _____.

If you *are ready to change*, **then** *close your eyes and go inside.*

This is a classic cause and effect statement. Most people will take whatever you tell them at face value. And it's easy to make logical/conscious use of a rational cause and effect so resistance is lowered.

The inordinately skeptical client may argue with every point. But **if you** *encourage even the skeptical client to experience hypnosis*, **then** *you have lasting success.* **If you** *confidently listen to a skeptical client*, **then** you can *simply recalculate as necessary.* You want to be in rapport with your client so agreement is necessary. In a pre-talk if you need to prime the pump to get the client's ideas flowing, you may find a particularly disagreeable person objecting to your suggestions. Nip that in the bud by teasingly saying something like, "Obviously I don't live your life. But you do! So let's hear your ideas. What is it that you are willing to do to achieve success"? **If you** *elicit their action steps and the benefits* derived from reaching the goal, **then** *you can fill in the blanks* of the language pattern.

On the subject of resistant clients, as you more clearly understand that your job as hypnotist is to gather enough information about the client to help them think differently about a problem, you will also understand that there is no failure. The client doesn't fail even if they answer a question or respond in a way that you didn't expect. It's feedback, useful added information. The hypnotist never fails either by using a pattern, a word, or a technique. It's just like cooking a pot of spaghetti. You probably already know that when you think the noodles are done, you pick up a strand of spaghetti and toss it against the wall. If it sticks, the noodles are ready to be drained. If it doesn't stick, you just keep cooking a little longer. There's no need to be frustrated with the attempt. It's just feedback on the cooking cycle. As soon as you discover that the noodles need a little more time on the stove, you just keep cooking. Then when the strand sticks, it's feedback to proceed to the colander.

For those who use an Elman-style induction, you know there is a sequence of convincers for the client/ testing for the hypnotist. No need to progress to the next step until the client "passes" this one. You can use that as feedback to repeat a previous step until there is enough rapport to proceed or you may choose a different technique to find a pathway for the client to allow that heightened state of receptivity/altered state of imagination.

As a hypnotist you want a depth and breadth of experience so you can use the feedback to recalculate and be flexible and knowledgeable enough to act accordingly. Feedback is invaluable so you can skillfully continue on the path or seamlessly move to a different pattern or technique. If the feedback says it's not working, anything different will give you a different outcome.

This pattern is easy enough to put into conversation and the patter works very well inside a hypnotic trance. The cause and effect doesn't even really have to make much sense so it allows for a wide variety of interesting outcomes.

If you *want that,* **then** *you can have it quickly.*

If you *direct your attention to your breathing,* **then** *you relax deeper on every exhale.*

If you *experience hypnosis,* **then** *you will discover how easy it is to make the change you want.*

If you *always answer your thirst first,* **then** *you find yourself releasing excess weight even faster.*

In order for the conscious mind to verify that the **then** part is true, the person will have had to DO the **if** part which is what you both want! That's an ultimate win-win.

My students have often said, "It's easy now to *address any client issue with the helpful use of magic words and language patterns.*"

8. _____ Said _____.

Milton Erickson once **said,** *"you can change easily and quickly"*

It was **Einstein who said "Problems cannot be solved with the same mindset that created them."** And *hypnosis works because you use a solution mindset.* I'm not suggesting anything to you, I'm just reporting what Einstein discovered. And in the last line of the above section I wasn't making a suggestion, (wink, wink) I was letting you know what my students have reported doing. There's really nothing there for your conscious mind to resist…go ahead…**try to resist**…as _you find yourself using the patterns all the time_!

Of course all the language patterns are such a comfortable part of communication that incorporating them into daily use is easy. Some **of my students say** they _choose one new pattern each week and weave it into conversations at every opportunity._ **Other students say**, "_It's so much fun I throw the whole pot of spaghetti at the wall_ at once to see what sticks!"

The use of quotes and stories and metaphors are classic and very effective ways of making suggestions embedded in what sounds or appears to be information. Hypnotists are hired to help people take the actions they need to take to make the necessary change(s) they want or need to make to get the life they desire. Doctors, nurses, coaches, motivators, teachers, parents, and indeed hypnotists are all in the business of persuasion. Thus all can make good use of language magic.

When I first discovered these language patterns, I practiced on everyone! And I still play word games just for fun sometimes. Like…the dreaded telemarketer. Mostly I just ignore the phone when it's a number I don't recognize, but occasionally when in a playful mood I'll actually talk with a stranger on the phone. I've been known to say things like, "Try to resist the urge to go ahead and hang up on me now! A person would make more calls by disconnecting this one now. If you do that, then we can both move on with our day. Sooner or later you will realize you need to remove my name from the calling list. You can imagine doing that now, can you not?" It's all fun and games until you get one of those telemarketers who is not allowed to hang up on a call.

Eventually even I can get too much of a good thing! But I have also had success in being removed from calling lists and after all, that was the end game in that encounter.

> This training should be required because **my friend Rick says,** *"Magic words and language patterns are the path to least resistance by the conscious mind."*

> **My aunt Betty says**, *"15 minutes walking in the sunshine every day keeps you healthy."*

> **My NLP trainer said,** *"You'll have fun as you find yourself using language patterns with everyone."* And I do!

> **What happens when you** *incorporate these powerful patterns into conversational hypnosis and ... trance-formation immediately?*

9. What Happens When You _____?

> **What happens when** you first *go into trance*?

You are already using this pattern every day whether you realize it or not. It may simply be happening automatically outside of conscious awareness such as changing lanes when you drive. People who use their turn signal when changing lanes (as ALL people should!) do it so automatically that it's happening without conscious intervention or awareness. As you drive to your location, just before changing lanes, you are wondering **what**

happens when you move over there and just before you take action you move that turn signal.

Just like Alice in Wonderland, you may have wondered many things. What happens when I eat this cake? What happens when a person neglects to pay a parking ticket? What happens when I stay out past curfew? What happens when a pretty girl accepts your dinner invitation? What happens when I achieve my goals? You encounter things to wonder about all day long. Go ask Alice, I think she'll know!

So if I ask a client "**What happens when you** *imagine zipping up your favorite jeans without a struggle?*" I'm just asking a question. For the conscious mind to come up with an answer the scene has to be played out in the imagination. You have to do it; no one can do it for you. Interestingly, once the scene plays out in the imagination, it's as if it's a rehearsed event. The subconscious doesn't know the difference between fact and a vividly imagined thought. Send the imagination into action on success steps and the details get worked out on their own.

The subconscious mind is very handy that way. Until you DECIDE to take a vacation, as an example, the mind can think about needing a break all it wants to with no results. But once you decide to take a vacation and you choose the destination, the thought becomes a fantasy and the subconscious mind goes into overdrive working out the details. Suddenly, almost by surprise, you are making arrangements such as how to get there, what to do while there, what to pack, etc.

Once your client has made a decision to change, and you ferret out the action steps and benefits from taking the action, you can make suggestions that lead to change and create the space for your client to rehearse the positive outcome while the details are set into motion. Go ahead and role play it. You be the client.

> **What happens when you** <u>imagine</u> *you are confidently and successfully hypnotizing for any issue?*

> **What happens when you** *use these language patterns* <u>*effortlessly*</u>*?*

> **What happens when you** <u>*believe*</u> *that you are good at helping people succeed?*

> **The more** you *use magic words and language patterns,* **the more** *you have* <u>*unlimited*</u> *confidence with every client.*

10. The more _____, the more _____.

> **The more** you *deeply consider* these patterns**, the more** *easily* your unconscious *integrates* them.

This language pattern is a way to express that two things vary together. Imagine a person in your office, reclined with their eyes closed and listening to your voice and the correlation is easily made as you say, "**The more** *you hear my voice,* **the more** *you go into trance now.*" You have stated a truism that the client can hear your voice with which they will readily agree. And the more they do that, the more they can relax or go into trance or imagine their success or whatever you suggest for them to do.

This pattern can be easily adapted to many variations. **The more** *you become relaxed*, the deeper you go and the deeper you go, **the more** *you relax now*. The assumption of relaxation and/or depth goes undisputed because the client can look for signs of relaxation or depth. Understand that depth is a vague term. Even the old school hypnotists who applied rules and created depth scales couldn't agree on the amount of depth it took to create various stages of hypnosis. And certainly the client likely doesn't know what it means. But the mystery then allows any sign (a breath, a tingle, a movement, lightness, heaviness…) to qualify as a belief that everything is going well. That's an excellent thought to have for someone in hypnosis.

On the subject of deepening, it's another variation of this pattern. And you probably already see the similarity.

> "I'll count from 10 down to one. With each number I count, you'll go deeper down. And on the count of 1, you will be at the most comfortable, safe and relaxing place you can imagine. <u>Begin</u> to *create that* <u>*now*</u>. **I wonder how** *you create a safe and comfortable place* **as** *you relax deeper with each number I count.* 10. Going deeper down. 9. **The more** *you can relax.* 8. **The more** *you let go* <u>*now*</u>. 7. 6. 5. Half way there now, getting closer to your safe and comfortable place. 4. 3. Almost there. 2. Just one number away from that safe and comfortable, relaxing place…<u>Imagine</u> *being there* <u>*now*</u>, <u>and</u> 1. Deep and comfortable and safe and relaxed."

As the numbers descend, the trance follows. The more you count down, the more deeply you in-trance your client because two things can vary at the same time (numbers and relaxation) so it makes sense to the Conscious and the Subconscious mind.

BTW—I count down to smaller numbers for deepening or regression. I count up to larger numbers for emerging or progression. But some hypnotists do it just the opposite. It doesn't matter either way—just be consistent with your choice to make it easy for your client to follow.

You don't even have to go "deeper". You or your client may prefer to go higher! Great! Reach up and commune with the higher power! Utilize what will work best for the client in your office. Remember, they don't know how hypnosis or your process is supposed to go. You are helping them discover it by suggesting things along the path. Keep it simple and congruent and utilize your client's values as leverage for the change

The more *you practice these language patterns,* **the more** *you have confidence to hypnotize clients without a script.* And **the more** *you hypnotize with confidence,* **the more** *you enjoy your success.* **The more** *you develop a solid foundation* with the patterns, **the more** *you discover how to adapt* them to your needs.

Chapter 18: Bonus Language Pattern

There are many language patterns, but the ten listed here will serve you very well to begin now. Still, let me give you one more as a bonus.

The more _____, the less_____.

In one of my favorite Facebook forums on hypnosis called Hypnotic Women, I asked for group members to share their favorite language patterns curious if one particular pattern or another got the most response. That didn't happen. There were many responses with a variety of adaptations. Jennifer Norris-Nielsen offered this variation on the more, the more pattern. She posted:

> "I use a lot of the more (than)…less (than) along with the more (than)…more (than). For example— "The more you used to _____, the less you find, now, that _____affects you." Or, "The more others _____ (problematic behavior, hot button), the more you (surprisingly-

a language pattern in itself (with curiously, interestingly, etc.) find you feel/can _____ (outcome/change/better feeling.)

Thank you, Jennifer. This is a perfect example of how you can take the patterns in this book and adapt or change or continue to investigate a variety of ways to use language to enhance your communications skills. You notice that using your own common sense and creativity expands your abilities in unlimited directions. It's exciting, isn't it?!

As you begin to use the various language patterns and the words that direct or suggest in and of themselves, you will find many ways to adapt this word and language magic and use it in all forms of persuasion and communication.

Chapter 19: Putting Magic Words & Language Patterns To Use

I recently finished teaching a Hypnosis Certification Training and, of course, I share the magic words and language pattern techniques with my students. Prior to this class session, one of my students, Deborah, had sent out three pitch letters to local businesses offering a self-hypnosis stress relief workshop for their employees. She'd been waiting two weeks and hadn't yet received a response from anyone. She realized pitch letters are a great way to practice using language patterns so she followed up with an email to her original contacts and this time included her new skills.

> "Sooner or later you realize the need for my stress relief workshop. The latest research shows the more employees relieve stress, the more productivity employers see in the workplace. And you can imagine the benefit of more productivity, can you not?

The sooner you call me; the more options you have for convenient scheduling. Try to resist the urge to call me today because relieving stress makes you feel so good!"

Deborah received two return calls the day after she sent this follow-up email. She gives credit to her new word skills for creating compelling compliance. This is one of many examples of the power of using these words and patterns in all you do.

With Your Clients

Let's pretend you have a client, Max, who is a self-proclaimed gym rat and now wants to enter a body-building contest. Max knows that with hard work he can build the necessary muscle, he's just not sure that he'll be confident enough to believe in himself. You discover through eliciting his personal trance words (*Personal Trance Words for Hypnotic Success at* www.KarenHand.com/Magic-Words) that when he is confident enough, Max will feel complete freedom and he believes that entering the contest will give him a chance to be rewarded for his hard work. Good luck finding a script that includes all those dynamics. And realize that on the phone Max's only request was to get some help to be motivated to work harder at the gym. You found out about the competition angle there in your office during the pre-talk. You could panic and try to adjust your workout script on the fly or you can imagine having fun as you expertly hypnotize your client on his individual issue.

Induce and deepen the trance...

"You and I both realize *you work hard to build a ripped body.* **A person can** *enjoy the rewards of hard work,* **can they not?**

Now, **imagine** *you entering a body-building competition.* **A person** deserves the accolades of their hard work, **do they not? The harder** *you work out at the gym,* **the more** *you are aware of your sculpted body.* **The more** *you notice your muscle definition,* **the more** *you gain strength and confidence to show off your efforts.*

Henry Ford once said, "If you believe that you can or if you believe that you can't, you are right." And believe in yourself because your proof can be seen in the mirror. **You probably already know** that for you, it's more than a belief, it's visible in a competitive world.

What happens when you **imagine** *you are now ready to compete?*

Imagine success!

You probably already know that building your body is the journey and showing it off is the rewarding destination. **If you** *build it,* **then you** *confidently anticipate success* and the freedom that comes with the praise for your efforts.

Sooner or later *you see yourself competing* on that stage <u>and now</u> **try to resist** your desire to *schedule more time in the gym* to increase definition<u> because</u> you *build confidence in your desire to compete.*

One of my clients wanted to eat fish during the Lenten season and actually enjoy the taste. Jim said he'd hated fish since his mother made him eat it when he was a kid. He also said his wife loves fish and he wanted to be able to take her out and enjoy her favorite seafood restaurant too.

We did a little age regression to check on his perception of the start of his problem and he was able to see a different perspective on the events which made him feel much more in control of his own desires. After the regression, there was patter to solidify the change that went something like this:

"<u>Because</u> you've had this experience today *you realize that you are in control of what you choose to eat*...nobody's forcing you. **I wonder how**...*you feel in control of your choices*...**can you imagine** deciding to *change your mind about things* that once seemed so certain. <u>But</u> <u>now</u> armed with better information...*You've changed your mind about many things*... **As a person grows,** *he changes, matures, becomes insightful.* <u>Once upon a time</u> you decided to walk instead of crawl...on your own *you worked out all of the balance issues necessary for success.* <u>And</u> **there you are deciding** to learn a new skill, adapting, changing, **looking at options**<u> and</u> *make the decision to make a healthy change for good.* **Sooner or later** notice…*you enjoy trying new things* <u>and</u> <u>as</u> *you find yourself looking forward to the adventure* of doing not only what you have to do…but *enjoying what you decide you ought to do.* <u>*Imagine*</u> *you at a time in your future as you make the decision to go ahead and enjoy your decision.* After you've done it once, it seems as though you've enjoyed it for a lifetime…<u>because</u> *that's what you want.*

The client's story becomes your narrative and the magic words and language patterns make it easy to successfully keep the patter going. That is how you go from being a "scriptnotist" to using Script-less Hypnosis. And, incidentally, after the session the client sent this text, "Took my wife to Bonefish tonight. Decided to order the Tilapia. And I really enjoyed it! Thanks!" Sometimes it is a "one-hit wonder" and he referred 5 other clients for various issues.

The language patterns can be used alone or strung together. They can be used in the intervention section of your session, recorded in an audio process, used as part of or in conjunction with metaphor(s), hypnosis or NLP techniques, or to follow age regression, forgiveness or parts work to solidify the change work. Imagine knowing these patterns so well you use them automatically. And you are probably already aware that the options for using the material in this book are unlimited. Try it on a maître d' the next time you want a good table and discover how successful you can be at getting what you want. And remember, if you get stuck at a lousy table…it's feedback…go back and notice how you delivered your suggestion or patter and change it accordingly the next time.

There is no way to discuss all the client issues that might come your way...otherwise, maybe I'd be writing a script book! But you can go to my website (www.KarenHand.com/magic-words) for a handy downloadable printable sheet of the magic words and language patterns. Students have said they keep the "cheat sheets" on their desk and have used the outline prompts until it becames second nature for them to use during sessions and all conversation.

This book is designed as an excellent foundation for hypnotic and persuasive language. This is certainly not the only list or even a complete list of all words and language patterns. But many previous students say this material is the groundwork for all suggestive patter used in their practice. Make this a liberal addition to all other trainings and notice how it dovetails perfectly with future trainings as well. After all, the words are magic and the language has a pattern to it. You will notice the hypnotic rhythm that is naturally formed as the language flows and the trance deepens. Try to resist the urge to use these patterns even in your social media posts and in conversation with your friends and family.

Adding these tools allows your direct suggestions for change to be wrapped into language that lowers resistance and efficiently crosses the critical factor for easy installation into the subconscious mind where imagination rules. As you know, the imagination knows no limits thus there are no limits to how you can use these magic words and language patterns! Take your unlimited imagination and you will easily expand your skill set and take your hypnosis practice to new heights!

Chapter 20: The Hidden Secret

The words and phrases themselves can easily fold into favorite scripts or patter you already have in use. And realize, you can increase your success even further as you expand your delivery skills of the language. Effective communication, especially for motivation and persuasion, also includes the voice and the body, two very special "tools" that can augment communication with inflection, tone, body language, facial expression, etc.

The voice is a versatile instrument that uses tempo and tone, volume and pitch. When you couple that with body language and facial expressions, you've got a lot of communication going on. Pitch and inflection add richness and depth to the voice for enhanced communication not limited to the hypnotic trance. The way you use your voice helps you deliver the meaning of your suggestion or message.

You use your voice effectively this way already in conversation. Now, you can use it on purpose to free yourself from the often held limiting belief that the hypnotic voice should be slow and mellow and as easy to listen to as an overnight easy listening radio DJ. The hypnotic voice can be soft or bossy/authoritarian. It can be rhythmic or staccato. It can be low or high. It can even be monotone. But remember, you don't want your clients to sleep in the chair. If they're truly asleep, they're probably not hearing your suggestions and unless you hope to get the suggestions for change into their mind through osmosis, it behooves you to keep them en-tranced with your vocal delivery and non-verbal cues as well.

When the client's eyes are wide open, their subconscious mind is picking up on cues from your body language, facial expressions and your voice. Their subconscious mind is checking for congruence. If your tone is saying one thing but your stance is saying another, rapport may be going out the window faster than your client can get out the door.

I have some acting and performance in my background so it comes naturally for me to "act out what I'm thinking and saying." If you tend to be less demonstrative, at the very least be aware of your facial expressions, gestures, shoulders, stance, etc. If you're saying something positive, make sure you're nodding your head, if only slightly. And try to resist noticing now when people are incongruent with their head. It's harder to believe someone who is shaking their head back and forth in a "no" style than someone who is smiling or nodding as they "sell" you something.

Even when your client's eyes are closed, congruence is important. So, go ahead and stand or sit up straight. Go into the physical as well as the vocal trance you want your client to achieve. Do it all over your body and with your voice. And there will be deeper rapport with your client even when they can't see you.

In the first week of my professional radio career, I was hired as a co-anchor for the morning newscasts. I was young and didn't care much about the news in those days, so I quickly imagined what a news person sounded like in my mind. In that first week, the program director told me I needed to lighten up. I sounded like I wanted to eat his children…so I lightened up! I was doing pretty well when a new program director pointed out that I would sound even better if I just "told the news as if I was telling a story to a friend over dinner." To me, that meant as if I was really talking to someone. It worked. And curiously, that advice works quite well now as I'm talking with my clients before, during, and after the trance. I stay in their zone and remain as congruent as possible head to toe with what I'm suggesting for my client. If I don't believe it, how can I motivate them to believe the suggestion?

Using the vocal instrument can really enhance the trance-formation for your client. Your voice interestingly becomes a non-verbal suggestion. If you're reading a story to a child, you likely speed up during action sequences, whisper to tell a secret, and smile or laugh when something is funny. Imagine now how that can enhance the experience for your client while they're in a heightened state of receptivity.

Inflection Exercise

Take a moment now to experience how much of a difference inflection can make to your message. Say the following sentence out loud, putting the inflection on the bold word. Each time you say it, you get a different meaning for the same sentence.

113

Emphasis	*Meaning*
I didn't say you should inflect more.	(Don't blame me!)
I **didn't** say you should inflect more.	(I said to use your voice congruently.)
I didn't **say** you should inflect more.	(But I did write it. And it was implied.)
I didn't say **you** should inflect more.	(I don't even know how much you inflect.)
I didn't say you **should** inflect more.	(I don't know your style maybe yours is fine.)
I didn't say you should **inflect** more.	(I said inflection and emphasis enhance the message.)
I didn't say you should inflect **more.**	(The way you do it may be fine.)

In each case, inflection and emphasis can change everything. So you can give even more clues about what you're wanting your client to experience by adding strategic emphasis to your voice.

Additionally, **upward inflection** tends to indicate a question, surprise or insincerity. **Downward inflection** is generally linked to confidence, power, or finality, period! (Pun intended and exclamation point for added emphasis. I hope you strongly inflected down!) No change in inflection may show indecisiveness or even a lack of interest. And this folds over into ending each and every sentence. Inflect up ONLY if you're really asking a question. Otherwise, inflect down or evenly. Use emphasis and inflection for power when you need it!

Vocal finesse is equally important on phone calls, speaking engagements, change work and hypnosis! It enhances communication by helping your client (or audience) understand your meaning and the substance of your message. Add in the language patterns and notice the impact.

Have you ever talked with a customer service agent on the phone and you just knew that they were tired and ready to go home? How did you feel about the service you were getting? Make sure your vocal representation is a convincer just like the Elman eye lock or any other convincer you use in sessions.

AND, there's nothing like a good pause to bring attention back to your voice. Remember elementary school when you were sitting in the back of the room giggling with your friend and suddenly the teacher stopped talking. That was an instant induction that took you directly to your protective part which automatically stopped your mouth and took your attention to the front of the room. Do not be afraid to pause to bring your client back to your voice or equally important to give them a chance to process new information.

Pitch, inflection, and pauses are handy tools to master and use as you talk with a client on the phone, during the pre-talk or wide-awake change work, and during hypnosis, in fact, in any form of communication. And, by the way, facial expressions and body language may not be important for the client when their eyes are closed in hypnosis but could be very important to your delivery. You must remain congruent. So even if no one can see you, don't sit there stoically when you want to convey a message of excitement. As they say, you go into the trance first and they will follow.

You can easily see a direct suggestion embedded in the language patterns. Play with your style on using those direct suggestions. Some say the language patterns work their own magic without highlighting the "command." Others prefer to pause one beat before the direct suggestion. Some vary their delivery throughout their communication. Develop your style so you can remain congruent. The receiver's subconscious mind is at work looking for all those same kind of clues that you pay close attention to as you're observing your client through the process. Give their subconscious mind a reason to easily go into and remain in rapport.

Let me take a moment to be very clear about something. No one has power over another human being. Every human has the right to accept or reject your suggestions. Even in the middle of a nice trance state, or a deep trance state, anyone has the right and the ability to reject your suggestions. People do not act against their value system or moral code. Trust me, if anyone had that actual power over non-suspecting others, they would hang out at the lottery office and convince new winners to turn over their money. If that actually happened, you'd know about it and a lot more people would be lining up to become hypnotists!

That being said, the elephant in the room is the question of whether or not people can be hypnotized to do anything against their will. No. Certainly hypnotic language can be used to manipulate someone into taking action. But it's not just the words themselves that have the power. It's the skillful use by a person who listens well and develops strong rapport, along with the willingness of the listener.

Manipulation itself is neither positive nor negative. It's just a word; the only magic is the meaning you give to the word. If you apply a negative connotation to it, that's your internal interpretation. A hypnotist who skillfully reframes (manipulates) a client's limited beliefs into better feeling actions is doing GOOD, are they not? A massage therapist who manipulates sore muscles is doing what you've paid for, aren't they? Using this information as part of the process of reframing your client's negative thinking is in their best interest and is an honorable use of manipulation.

Realize inroads can be made into someone's pattern of thinking when any person, hypnotist or not, taps into basic needs. A used car salesman knows the person who walked onto the lot wants a car. The more rapport that is developed with the prospective client, the more information is divulged. And the salesman who actively listens carefully can steer the buyer...to maybe the most expensive car that fits their needs for safety, and reliability and affordability. But understand, even the best used car salesman can't make a person who is just walking by the dealership buy a car or anything else that they didn't want in the first place. You can insert "gang leader" or "cult leader" instead of used car salesman here. No one, even with the use of magic words and hypnotic language patterns, can make a person do something they don't want to do or value in some way.

That's why it's much less successful to "proselytize" hypnosis. If you walk up to a group of smokers on a street corner and give them your business card, do you really think they will become clients? They're not looking for ways to quit at that moment. When someone who is actually looking for help to stop smoking or make any change sees your ad or website or workshop, they then choose to become a client. And then as you establish rapport, and skillfully use language with the artful application of successful techniques you can help make the desired change easy for the client.

I trust you are excited to begin implementing these words and patterns, and know that you use your power for good. Imagine using this secret sauce for more successful sessions and a more profitable practice!

A person can go script-less can they not, because simply using the magic words and language patterns helps the client change limits into success. And **the client-centered hypnotist uses every available avenue to help their clients** reach the goals they're seeking**, do they not**?

Try to resist using the language patterns on your spouse or kids or co-workers to practice and understand covertly changing outcomes. After you practice you realize how easy it is and you notice more confidence in your ability to include some magic (and maybe a new game for you) in your work with clients. With practice it becomes automatic for you. But, if you prefer further training in magic language or using Your Hypnotic Voice to its fullest advantage, contact Karen@KarenHand.com or call 312-315-2100.

It doesn't matter if you have the dulcet tones of Morgan Freeman or a voice like Minnie Mouse, developing your vocal instrument to match your intention will increase your success with communication.

Chapter 21: Go And Do

Theoretically, it is possible to build a house using only some lumber plus a hammer and nails. But imagine the things you can build when you have additional tools. When you add a saw and a power drill and screws and a level, etc. then you greatly expand your options for a successful creation...you could build a castle!

These magic words and language patterns are additional tools for you to add to your tool chest. You may choose to incorporate all of the techniques immediately. Or you may choose to use one new word and/or language pattern every day or week or month. Either way, sooner or later, these language patterns become as natural as any other part of speech. And the more you use them, the more success you notice immediately.

Have fun practicing on your friends or co-workers. They won't even notice and you can covertly monitor your success and expand the use of these magic words and language patterns to the fullest extent that you can make them work for you.

The "secrets" to success are new tools and skills to implement in your practice. As you become comfortable, you will witness your clients' success and feel more competent when no script is handy or appropriate. And now you understand that spending time on learning these magic words and language patterns is a win-win for your clients and you, so relax and enjoy. And go and do!

The only limits to your creativity and your success are the limits you place on your own imagination.

Appendix: Bonus Material

EGO STRENGTHENING

The Hartland Ego Strengthening Script is one of the most often seen and used Classical Hypnosis Scripts. Dr. John Hartland was a renowned British Psychiatrist in the 1960's and 70's. He credited his "general direct suggestion" script with a 70% success rate among patients in "short term therapy" meaning less than 20 sessions. He claimed the use of just this script had such wide-reaching success because of its vague and general nature allowing his patient to do their own internal work. You can find the full unedited version simply by googling The Hartland Ego-Strengthening Script.

I've chosen to include here for you (with permission of course) Jason Linett's updated and all-positive version of the Hartland Script. This following is from Jason's Hypnosis Certification Manual. Because I like his approach, I think you will find it useful as well.

JASON'S ALL-POSITIVE EGO STRENGTHENING

- As you walk out that door today, you begin to find yourself feeling physically stronger and fitter. MORE alert, MORE wide-awake, and MORE energetic.

- You begin to find yourself feeling SO deeply interested in whatever you are doing, that your mind is MUCH LESS preoccupied with the challenges of yesterday, and MUCH MORE aware of your abilities today.

- Every day your nerves become stronger and steadier. Your mind is calmer and clearer, more composed, more peaceful and at ease.

- You begin to think MORE clearly, concentrate MORE easily, and your memory improves as you see things in their true perspective, without allowing them to get out of proportion.

- Every day you find yourself becoming emotionally much calmer, MUCH MORE peaceful and at ease.

- You feel a greater feeling of personal well-being, a greater feeling of personal safety and security, MORE than you have felt in a long, long time.

- You begin to discover much more confidence in yourself, MUCH MORE confidence in your ability to do, not only what you have to do each day, but MUCH MORE confidence in your ability to do whatever you ought to be able to do, and to do it easily, optimistically, and happily.

- Because of this, every day you feel more and more independent, more able to stick up for yourself, _especially when it's to yourself_, to hold your own, no matter how difficult or trying things may be.

- And, because all these things will begin to happen, not because I say so, not because of some wonderful words I know how to say, but simply because it's the nature of who you are. You begin to feel much happier, much more contented. Much more cheerful, much more optimistic, and it really is true, every day in every way you will do better and better.

This is an all-positive handling of Hartland's Ego Strengthening technique modeled after an idea from Ron Eslinger. This information can be used in ANY advanced hypnotic intervention, whether it be future pacing, age regression, parts therapy, forgiveness, etc.

For a printable copy of Jason's patter scripts go to

Www.KarenHand.com/Magic-Words

123

EMERGE

I also include for you Jason Linett's adaptation of the Hartland Script for an emerging technique. I provide this to show how versatile ANY word, pattern, script or information can be if you'll incorporate it into your stream of knowledge and apply it where it works best for your client.

From Jason Linett's Hypnosis Certification Manual:

And now as I count forward from 1-5, you'll allow that energy to rise back up in you.

And as you walk out the door today, you'll notice yourself looking for even the smallest signs of success…. you'll always get what you're looking for. And success breeds more success.

1. Now, you find yourself feeling physically stronger and fitter. MORE wide-awake, and MORE energetic. MUCH LESS preoccupied with the challenges of yesterday, and MUCH MORE aware of your abilities today. Your nerves stronger and steadier. Your mind calmer and clearer, more composed, more peaceful and at ease.

2. You realize you think MORE clearly, concentrate MORE easily, and you see things in their true perspective, without allowing them to get out of proportion. Every day finding yourself becoming emotionally much calmer.

3. You feel a greater feeling of personal well-being, safety and security. You begin to discover much more confidence in your ability to do what you have to do each day, and MUCH MORE confidence in your ability to do whatever you ought to be able to do, easily, optimistically, and happily.

4. And because you are aware these things are happening, not because I say so, not because of some wonderful words I know to say, but simply because it's the decision you made for yourself. You begin to feel much more contented. Much more cheerful, optimistic as every day you do better and better.

5. Eyes open, refreshed, alert, feeling good.
Jason Linett copyright 2015

Thank you for reading and I look forward to staying connected! Go to www.KarenHand.com/Magic-Words to download your list of Magic Words and Language Patterns now!

Acknowledgements

Words have always tickled my fancy, and I hope you now start (or continue) a deep appreciation and respect for the power of words and language. There have been many influences along my hypnosis career and I want to give a shout out here to a few of those people who helped along the literary path of this journey.

Cal Banyan asked me to be a regular contributor to his 5-Path® Journal which was my first professional writing experience in this field. NLP trainer Dr. William Horton introduced me to the fascinating game of word play to help affect change. Melissa Tiers' vast knowledge and presentation skills (first witnessed at a National Guild of Hypnotists Convention in Massachusetts) connected the dots between hypnosis and neuroscience and, like me, she respects the conscious mind in the hypnosis process. Fellow Chicago hypnotists Larry Garrett and Carm Blacconiere have always provided recognition and encouragement to use the stage and the page to pass along what I have learned. Book-writing workshops presented by Michael DeSchalit (at the HypnoThoughtsLive Convention in Las Vegas) and Shelley Stockwell-Nicholas (at the Mid-America Hypnosis Conference in Chicago) made the whole process seem less daunting and more possible. Jess Marion, Shawn Carson, and Sarah Carson model the level of educational excellence I expect of myself and provided the first visual image of the book(s) in my dreams. But it was Linda Otto who actually solidified this book when she interviewed me for the International Association of Counselors and Therapists "Ask The Professional" Column. The topic was magic words and language patterns and after completing the interview, I told her it was the impetus for making this the first book in the "Handbook for Scriptless Hypnosis" series. And finally, my editor, Kelly Epperson, has been a wonderful accountability partner and cheerleader. I'm hoping it leads to the full table of books that we're already excitedly discussing!

Hypnosis is an evolving art and science and there is no one single technique that works every time. I'm grateful for every trainer I've had the privilege to know, watch, or read, and I absolutely understand that the learning never stops! It's wonderful what you can discover when you are open to learning new things, isn't it?

ABOUT THE AUTHOR

Karen Hand is a Board Certified Hypnotist and Instructor, NLP Master Practitioner, and EFT Facilitator. She has been honored by numerous national organizations for her communication expertise and hypnosis excellence and has served on the board of several professional groups and organizations.

Karen was a morning radio personality and News Director on the most popular contemporary music station in Chicago for 30 years and hosted the #1 rated relationship advice show *Private Lives* where (along with Dr. Kelly Johnson) she enlightened an entire generation of Chicagoans on issues rarely discussed in public. She couldn't help sharing her knowledge even then as an instructor of contemporary writing and delivery at Columbia College in Chicago.

Karen is a sought-after speaker and instructor. She uses her communication skills to train and certify hypnotists and NLP Practitioners and has a private practice in Chicago. Karen also instructs doctors, nurses, first responders, teachers, coaches, parents and sales people in groups and one-on-one in the fine art of conversational persuasion for communication success.
For a current training schedule go to www.KarenHand.com.

Karen invites you to call her at 312-315-2100 and please feel free to email her at Karen@KarenHand.com and tell her about your success.

Made in United States
North Haven, CT
21 September 2022

24368535R00075